Writing for Life and Ministry

Writing for Life and Ministry

A Practical Guide to the Writing Process for Teachers and Preachers

Brandon J. O'Brien

Redeemer City to City

MOODY PUBLISHERS

CHICAGO

Scripture taken from the NEW AMERICAN STANDARD BIBLE®, Copyright © 1960, 1962, 1963,
1968, 1971, 1972, 1973, 1975, 1977, 1995 by The Lockman Foundation.
Used by permission.

All emphasis in Scripture has been added.

A version of the content in this book was previously published as a writing course offered through
Redeemer City to City.

Edited by Amanda Cleary Eastep
Interior Design: Ragont Design
Cover design and imagery by Alastair Sterne

All websites and phone numbers listed herein are accurate at the time of publication but may
change in the future or cease to exist. The listing of website references and resources does not imply
publisher endorsement of the site's entire contents. Groups and organizations are listed for informa-
tional purposes, and listing does not imply publisher endorsement of their activities.

Library of Congress Cataloging-in-Publication Data

Names: O'Brien, Brandon J., author.
Title: Writing for life and ministry : a practical guide to writing for
  publication / Brandon O'Brien, Redeemer City to City.
Description: Chicago : Moody Publishers, [2020] | Includes bibliographical
  references. | Summary: "No matter how you feel about writing,
  approaching a project can be overwhelming. In Writing for Life and
  Ministry you'll learn how to plan, draft, and revise to effectively
  develop your skills. And by following the included exercises, you'll be
  ready to tackle that writing project with confidence"-- Provided by
  publisher.
Identifiers: LCCN 2020004642 (print) | LCCN 2020004643 (ebook) | ISBN
  9780802419767 (paperback) | ISBN 9780802498694 (ebook)
Subjects: LCSH: Christian literature--Authorship--Handbooks, manuals, etc.
  | Christian literature--Publishing--Handbooks, manuals, eetc.
Classification: LCC BR44 .O37 2020 (print) | LCC BR44 (ebook) | DDC
  808.0202/42--dc23
LC record available at https://lccn.loc.gov/2020004642
LC ebook record available at https://lccn.loc.gov/2020004643

Originally delivered by fleets of horse-drawn wagons, the affordable paperbacks from D. L. Moody's
publishing house resourced the church and served everyday people. Now, after more than 125 years
of publishing and ministry, Moody Publishers' mission remains the same—even if our delivery
systems have changed a bit. For more information on other books (and resources) created from a
biblical perspective, go to: www.moodypublishers.com or write to:

Moody Publishers
820 N. LaSalle Boulevard
Chicago, IL 60610

1 3 5 7 9 10 8 6 4 2

Printed in the United States of America

Contents

1

Introduction (or A Different Kind of Writing Book)

These days everyone is a "content creator." This is because, as one marketing consultant explains, "every organization must produce valuable, education based content in order to compete in business today."[1]

The same is true for churches, nonprofits, ministries, and seminaries: just about every organization has to produce written material of some sort. And for that reason, writing is increasingly considered a normal part of many ministry leaders' regular responsibilities. They write blogs or newsletters for their congregations or networks, share lessons for other practitioners, and write books to extend their preaching or teaching ministry to a broader audience. Sometimes organizations encourage these projects and reduce a leader's other responsibilities to make time for writing. Sometimes a leader's writing is a personal ambition and not formally part of the job description. Either way, writing increasingly is an important milestone in many people's ministry careers.

So if everyone is expected to write, does that mean everyone is a writer?

To quote one of my favorite television characters: "Yes, I suppose, if we broaden the definition of writer to those who can spell."[2]

The real answer is, of course, no. Just because we are expected to write doesn't mean we suddenly become adept at writing or more enthusiastic about it.

That's where this book comes in. The purpose of this book is to help you become a better and more confident writer. I assume you have some responsibility, or desire, to produce curricula, Bible studies, fundraising newsletters, blog posts, supporter updates, maybe even a book. And while you may have ambitions to write or feel called to write, I suspect it's just as likely that you feel pressure to write. Someone (your congregation, denomination, professional network, conference attendees) has asked you to write, but the idea intimidates you. You say, "The thing is, I'm not really a writer." Maybe you have a project in mind but have written, to date, exactly zero words. Maybe you've gotten started and the words are all terrible and you just want to give up.

If you're feeling any of this, don't worry. If you need help figuring out what to write about, who you are writing for, how to get started, and how to see a project through to the end, this book is for you.

Put another way, the goal of this guide is to demystify the writing process by treating writing like a craft. In any craft—take woodworking, for example—there are tools, processes, and best practices that can turn a brand-new beginner into a competent craftsman. Over time, as a competent craftsman becomes more comfortable with the tools and processes, he becomes a master craftsman.

In the same way, there are tools, processes, and best practices for writing that can help you grow from wherever you are now as a writer to be both more confident *and* more competent in your work.

How This Book Is Different

Most books, guides, workshops, blog posts, and conferences about writing—at least, the ones I've read and attended—typically emphasize a couple of things: either self-expression or getting published. These are both important topics. Guides that encourage self-expression are helpful because at some point every writer has to summon at least enough courage and confidence to start writing. Overcoming the fear of a blank page or the fear of criticism is essential. But it's the very beginning of the process. There's a lot more to writing than self-expression.

At the same time, learning to build a platform, connect with an audience, and find your place in the market are important, too, especially for a writer who's trying to make a living or supplement their income by writing. But being published is the end of the process. There's a lot more to writing than simply "getting discovered."

There's another type of resource out there that addresses style and other sentence-level mechanics of good writing. Strunk and White's *Elements of Style*, a classic desk reference for writers, editors, and students for decades, falls into this category. And it's an essential resource. But it assumes a good many things, including that you are writing and need to get better.

But what if you're *not* writing and need to get *started*? What if you feel comfortable preaching, teaching, or speaking but freeze up in front of a blank screen? What if people keep telling you, "You should write a book!" and you have no idea what you would write about and who would even read it?

This book will help you answer those questions.

Part 1 will help you identify your unique contribution—what you ought to write about—as well as your specific audience—who you ought to write for.

Part 2 will walk you through the writing process in three stages:

1. **Planning:** choosing your specific topic and what you have to say about it

2. **Drafting:** getting words on an empty page

3. **Revising:** turning those words on the page into a composition you are proud to share publicly

That's it. That's the whole process. And it may sound too simple. But if you internalize this process, follow it, and learn to trust it, your writing will improve. I can't promise your life will change or that you'll find fame and fortune. But you'll write better.

"The" Process and "Your" Process

Please understand I'm not trying to reduce the creative process to a series of steps that guarantee results. There are no three easy steps to writing the next great American novel or best-selling self-help book or ministry manifesto. The reason for emphasizing the process is that you will become discouraged at some stage while writing. Guaranteed. If you don't realize that stage is a predictable part of the process and that *everyone* gets discouraged here, you will give up. And that would be a shame.

Learning the process and trusting the process takes some of the anxiety out of the work. That's ultimately what I'm trying to do—to remove some non-essential anxiety from your life. You're welcome.

Emphasizing the process also is not intended to suggest that writers are, in the end, just paragraph-producing vending machines. There's a difference between *the* process and *your* process. Here's an example from a different creative process: cooking.

Imagine two people who enjoy cooking. One likes to follow a recipe the first few times she makes a new dish to get a sense of the basics before she starts to experiment. She likes to measure everything carefully first. She washes all the dishes and starts with a clean kitchen, organizes all the ingredients at the beginning, and cleans up as she goes. The other, God bless him, takes a different approach. He may glance over a couple of recipes to get a lay of the land, and then he'll wing it. Instead of measuring carefully, he works in pinches, dashes, and smidges. He leaves open containers and empty cartons and dirty utensils on every available flat surface until whatever he's making goes into the oven to bake or onto the stove to simmer. Then he addresses the mess.

Each cook works differently. Both ways, food ends up on the table. Both meals taste great. And, when it's all said and done, both cooks follow the same basic process:

They plan—make decisions about what they're going to make and how.

They make—chop, mix, proof, julienne, etc.

They refine—season, finish, present, eat.

Even though the individual approaches are different (and probably cause the other person stress), both are working the same fundamental process.

The same is true for writing. Every writer works uniquely. Some draft detailed outlines, color-code notecards, carefully organize a digital filing system, and then systematically draft page after page of prose before making their final revisions. Others work from hastily sketched outlines—or none at all—or thoughts and ideas recorded in fourteen different notebooks, journals, napkins, or grocery receipts all over the apartment, never to be found again. They dash out sentences or paragraphs here and there, until, eventually, it all comes together as an actual document. Some read and talk and read and talk and bore friends and family with the intricate details of their "writing project" long before—*eons* before, if you ask the friends and family—they type a word of it. Some work best in the morning, some at night; some in short daily increments, some in long reclusive weekend retreats. No matter what, when it's all said and done, everyone plans, drafts, and revises, if each in their own way.

The purpose of this guide is to *familiarize* you with the process—plan, draft, revise. It includes exercises to help you *internalize* the process—trust it and own it—so that *the* process becomes *your* process.

Instead of focusing on self-expression or getting published, we're going to spend our time getting better at the craft of writing. We'll talk about developing habits and improving self-awareness. The good news is, the process we unpack in the pages that follow will give you greater confidence and competence, not only in writing, but in any creative work you may do—from preaching to project management. If we can demystify the process, we can master it. And then you can confidently start and finish projects that intimidated you before.

Fine. But who are you and why should I listen?

I've been writing professionally for about a dozen years. In that time, I've written books and articles and blog posts, email newsletters, sermons and book reviews, a doctoral dissertation—just about anything you might need to write. Which is to say that I have more than a decade of experience figuring out who I am as a writer, who I write for, and practicing and personalizing the process.

More relevant for you at the moment, I have coached first-time writers, many of whom are ministry practitioners. I did this first as an editor for *Leadership Journal* (a former publication from Christianity Today International) and later as a service for publishers who were publishing first-time authors. Now it's a key part of my job at Redeemer City to City. Our organization's vision is to see the great cities of the world transformed by the gospel of Jesus Christ. One ingredient in city transformation is locally produced and contextualized materials that help leaders communicate the gospel to the hearts of their neighbors. That is, one ingredient is competent writing. Competent writing produced by people who don't necessarily feel like competent writers. On every habitable continent of the planet, I meet with groups of pastors to help them determine their unique contribution, understand their target reader, and internalize the creative process. The material in this book has empowered ministry leaders in Europe and Asia, Africa and Latin America, to find their writer's "voice" and serve their communities confidently. It has been my experience that the material applies across cultures and in numerous languages.

For this reason, I'm confident this resource can help you too. There are exercises throughout the book because the only way to improve in writing is to *write*. You'll read a little and write a lot. The exercises are designed to be most helpful if you apply them to an actual, specific project. So if there's a writing project you've been putting off indefinitely, consider pulling it out of the drawer, blowing the dust off, and using it as the focus of your activities in this guide. Each chapter and activity will move you one step closer to completion.

Whether you're writing because you want to or because you have to, I'm glad you're here. Let's make something great together.

2

·

I Can Preach
(or Teach or Coach . . .).
Why Can't I Write?

You should see me swing a golf club. Knees bent, feet shoulder-width apart. I step into the swing, rotate my hips, roll my wrists. If I manage to make contact with the ball, it rolls a few feet and stops in the tee box. Usually I miss the ball completely. The problem is, I grew up playing baseball, and I can't shake the instinct to swing a golf club like a baseball bat. Some people can do both. Good for them. I can't.

People are often surprised to discover a similar dynamic at work in communication. They have years of experience with public speaking and are quite good at it. They can preach down the rafters, keep a classroom full of uninterested teenagers hanging on every word, and walk a cohort of adults through the most tedious of professional training exercises with joy. But when they sit down in a quiet room alone, stared down by a blank white page and blinking cursor, they feel helpless.

They think, *I can teach* (or preach or coach or whatever). *Why can't I write?*

Others feel the opposite. They can churn out coherent, compelling pages of print or blog posts all day long, but they panic in front of real live humans.

Very few people move confidently between oral and written communication. There are notable exceptions, to be sure. But odds are that the celebrity preacher you love to listen to and whose books sell gobs of copies didn't actually write the books. Odds are a team of people who are experts in written communication helped a great deal or did it for him, so that the gifted *oral* communicator could appear to be an expert writer. This process is called "ghostwriting." It's a common practice and not a nefarious one, but it is invisible. It gives the impression that the speaker/author is gifted at all forms of communication, which may not be the case.

Furthermore, it creates a set of expectations to live up to. Increasingly, those of us in ministry are expected to be good at both. If you are a popular speaker with a big or growing platform, it won't be long before a publisher asks you to write a book. Maybe your own congregation will ask. If you lead retreats or conferences or teach or consult and people are helped and encouraged by your work, someone will say to you, "You should really write a book about this." If you are in ministry, chances are you will someday feel pressure to write, whether you aspire to or not.

I don't think everyone should write a book. But you will have to write *something* that you don't want to write or don't feel qualified to write—a newsletter, a blog post, a Bible study. If you serve in ministry, you likely have some ability and some level of comfort communicating orally. And it may be that one of the reasons you don't write more or don't like to write is because it's *hard*, or unnatural, or exhausting. I get it. That's normal. You're not wrong or defective. Over the years I've worked with lots of pastors and ministry leaders who start to write and feel discouraged. "I preach every week. That's like writing a new chapter of a book every week. I thought I would be good at this. I thought this would be easier. I don't know where to start."

Writing can be difficult for every new writer. But people who communicate orally for a living—pastors and teachers, for example—will feel the differences keenly when they start writing because shifting from preparing and delivering presentations to writing articles or blog posts is a bit like switching from baseball to golf. Both involve smacking a white ball with a long stick. But the tools are different, and using them correctly requires different techniques.

Some Differences between Speaking and Writing

There are significant differences between speaking and writing, and switching between the two presents challenges.

1. A different set of tools available—and not available

Acclaimed American writer Kurt Vonnegut once said, "When I write, I feel like an armless legless man with a crayon in his mouth."[1] If you are a speaker who is beginning in writing, you might feel similarly.

When you speak, you have gestures, tone of voice, volume, presentation slides, video clips, a PA system, screens, live music, handouts—snacks—and other means of capturing and keeping people's attention, expressing shades of meaning, and signaling humor or sarcasm. Those tools are *not* at your disposal in print. And you can't just make up for those things with bold type, all caps, and exclamation marks. (Seriously. You can't. Please don't.)

2. A different relationship with the audience

When you speak, at least in your own familiar context, you know the people well. You know what they find funny or helpful. You can change course in the middle of your presentation when you read expressions or body language and realize that something is unclear or didn't land right. In a real sense, the audience is helping you create the oral presentation in real time. With writing, you have to deliver a finished product to an invisible and possibly unknown audience. They don't know you. They may not be inclined to give you the benefit of the doubt. They can't read your mind and you can't read their faces.

The only constant in the shift from live to print delivery is you.

3. A different priority

Writing well requires time—time for brainstorming, time for preparing, time for drafting, time for revision. Lack of time is a challenge for most people who write. If writing is not your full-time job, there will always be something more urgent and perhaps more important for you to do instead of writing. A friend or church member will need counseling. A student crisis will need attending. An email will require a response. Crises crop up at the most inopportune times. If writing is something you do *in addition to* your job, you will have to make a conscious effort to prioritize your writing time.

In short, being a competent and confident preacher or teacher doesn't necessarily translate into being a competent and confident writer. You can become one, for sure. But you'll have to acquire some new tools and unlearn some habits.

Some Similarities between Speaking and Writing

When you consider the similarities between speaking and writing, you'll see how your experience as an oral communicator has its advantages. There are several ways speaking experience can make you a better writer.

1. As a communicator already, you know your audience well.

Understanding your audience is one of the writer's most important jobs. If you're a pastor, for instance, you definitely know your audience. You perform their weddings and funerals. You baptize or dedicate their children. You pray beside their hospital beds and celebrate their milestones. You have counseled them in their traumas. You have helped them overcome their addictions. Likely, these people also make up your readership, or at least part of it. If, as you write, you keep in mind the known needs and pain points of the people you serve, you'll be much more likely to connect with readers.

2. Your experience developing sermons and lessons and workshops has given you an education in the creative process.

By now you've probably discovered the answers to a few questions about your work habits that every writer needs to answer eventually: What time of day are you most productive? Where do you work best? How do you generate ideas, identify the strongest ones, and develop them into a presentation?

It took me years of writing to learn the answers to questions like these. You may know your answers already.

3. You have a voice.

Many new writers feel a great deal of pressure to write in a clear and distinct voice. They want the kind of writing style a reader can recognize immediately as belonging to them. This distinct voice is made up of the writer's tone, choice of words, and turns of phrase. It takes many writers years to develop their voice.

An advantage of speaking and teaching is that you have likely found your voice. All that's left to do now, as journalist and best-selling author William Zinsser puts it, is to "Relax and say what you want to say."[2] This is easier said than done, of course. It will take some time to figure out how to translate your voice into print. But if you are accustomed to speaking, you already have something to say, you say it regularly, and you say it in your own unique way.

So take heart. Some of what we do together may be new to you. Some of it may be familiar. But believe me when I say: You can do this.

The most important step is simply to start doing it.

●

Do It: Reflect on Your Experience

What kind of experience, if any, do you have with preparing presentations, "talks," lessons, workshops, etc.?

_____

_____

_____

_____

_____

_____

_____

_____

What is easiest for you in this process? What's hardest?

_____

_____

_____

_____

_____

_____

_____

_____

_____

_____

_____

_____

What do you find the most fulfilling? Why?

_____

_____

_____

_____

_____

_____

_____

_____

_____

_____

_____

Do It: Write Your Bio in Third Person

We've started talking a bit about your strengths and weaknesses. In the next section, we'll focus more on what makes you *you*—how to determine your unique contribution. To get the ball rolling, dedicate thirty minutes or so to this exercise:

Write a short personal biography in the third person (writing in third person means referring to yourself by your first/given name). Be sure to include the following information:

- Your name

- Your current job/title/position

- A brief review of your experience, education, and professional credentials

- Who lives in your house or apartment with you: spouse? children? pets? in-laws?

If what you are writing feels flat or boring, consider answering these questions/prompts:

- Write about your hobbies or interests. What do you do to relax?

- Share your personal ambitions and aspirations. How do you want to be remembered by history?

- Relate an experience that proved you were a proper adult. (Maybe, for example, you found yourself surprisingly excited about the sale price of laundry detergent.)

Don't worry about submitting a polished document. Write for *no more than* twenty minutes.

Example:

Brandon J.O'Brien (PhD, Trinity Evangelical Divinity School) is Director of Content Development and Distribution for Redeemer City to City, where he coordinates, edits, and shepherds writing projects with Pastor Timothy Keller and urban church planters around the world. Brandon has served in pastoral ministry, worked in publishing, authored a few books, and taught for state and Christian colleges and universities. He and his wife Amy and their two children live in Uptown Manhattan. They enjoy good food, good company, and exploring New York City.

_____

_____

_____

_____

_____

_____

_____

_____

_____

_____

_____

_____

_____

PART 1

The Writer and the Reader

3

• — — — — • — — — — •

Define the
Relationship

S trip everything else away—and I mean everything, down to the
pencils and keyboards—and writing is fundamentally about
two human beings in a relationship: the writer and the reader.

Novelist Stephen King characterizes this relationship (not surprisingly) as engaging in telepathy. The writer, he says, sits in his or
her "sending place"—an office or study or kitchen table—and the
reader sits in his or her "receiving place," and the writer sends the
reader a message across time and space.

> Look—here's a table covered with a red cloth. On it is a cage
> the size of a small fish aquarium. In the cage is a white rabbit
> with a pink nose and pink-rimmed eyes. In its front paws is
> a carrot-stub upon which it is contentedly munching. On its
> back, clearly marked in blue ink, is the numeral 8. Do we see
> the same thing?[1]

Allowing for variances, of course, we *do* see the same thing.
We see what King wants us to see. We see it clearly and vividly.
This is extraordinary. "We're not even in the same *year* together,"

King writes, "let alone the same room . . . except we *are* together. We're close."[2]

The writer and the reader, participating across time and space in an act of telepathy. Imagine that.

William Zinsser uses different language to communicate a similar message. Fundamental to all good writing is the "personal transaction" between the writer and the reader. The deeply personal nature of this relationship is one thing that makes writing so scary. It requires deep vulnerability from the writer, who is "driven by a compulsion to put some part of [himself] on paper."[3]

Managing this relationship between the writer and the reader requires deep sensitivity and not a little self-awareness.

We're spending time here because what most aspiring writers *think* they need is better strategies for churning out pages, a bigger platform for reaching more people, or their first big break. What most writers *actually, really* need is to remember that writing is a personal transaction—an act of telepathy—and so, fundamentally, what they need to do is to wrestle with these questions:

1. Who are you, *really*, and why do you want to write?

2. Who are you writing for, *ultimately*, and what do you want to do for them?

Your answers to these questions help you articulate your 1) unique contribution and 2) your specific reader.

The most effective writers have a clear sense of both parties in this transaction at all times. Effective writers know themselves. They know what they have to say and how they want to say it. They have a clear style and voice because they have learned, with practice, to write naturally. And they have realized, at some point, that they can't please every critic or reviewer so they have to write for themselves.

At the same time, effective writers also have a clear idea who their reader is and how that reader will respond to and resonate with what they're reading. They understand that reader's sense of humor, ambitions, and anxieties. The best writers don't just have something to say; they also know how they need to say it to be true to themselves and to connect with their reader at the same time.

When I was a magazine editor, it always set off alarms for me when an aspiring writer would tell me, "I can write about anything you need me to write about. The subject doesn't matter." They were trying to be flexible, and I understand where the comment was coming from. Even so, that statement always indicated that I was talking with a writer who didn't understand the dynamics between the author and the reader. It showed me they didn't understand the nature of the transaction. They wanted to be *published*. They weren't motivated, primarily, by the desire to send an important message to a receptive reader.

Understanding yourself as a writer and understanding the needs of your reader are lifelong pursuits.

There are two exercises in Part 1 designed to help you make these important decisions.

The first exercise (chapter 4) will help you decide what topic or topics you should consider writing about by helping you reflect on what subjects you are interested in, what you are knowledgeable about, and on what subjects you have unique perspective. This is not the sum total of who you are as a writer, but it's a good start. The goal of the exercise is to help you identify, somewhat objectively, your unique contribution.

The second exercise (chapter 5) will help you identify your primary reader. We're all tempted to write for "everyone." We want "everyone" to like our stuff. The problem is, if you write for "everyone," it's highly likely your work won't resonate with anyone.

It will be too generic. That means you have to identify or choose a specific reader for your writing and get to know them deeply. Your reader may change somewhat from project to project, or they may stay the same for all your work. Either way, you need to have a clear idea who you're writing for. You should be able to see them in your mind's eye as you write. The second exercise will help you do that.

You can complete these exercises on your own. But it would be enormously helpful for you to share your results with someone you trust. The people who know you best can offer helpful insights into all the questions you'll be wrestling with in these exercises.

Please accept this gentle reminder that you'll only benefit from this material if you put in the work. Set aside plenty of time to complete the exercises and reflect on them. The time you invest now will pay off in the long term.

Do It: Know Thyself

An important part of your transaction with your reader is your posture as a writer. Do you view yourself as an expert whose job is to educate the eager reader? Do you view yourself as one of the guys or a hot mess whose job is to put your arm around the reader's shoulder and talk as equals? A future exercise will help you think about the subject matter that makes up your unique contribution. This one is intended to get you thinking about your posture in the writer/reader relationship. Circle or highlight any that apply.

A. I view myself primarily as:

Educator	Parent	Encourager
Prophet	Mentor	Pastor
Counselor	Guide	Friend
Teacher	Fellow pilgrim	Coach

B. I am primarily concerned about or interested in:

_____

_____

_____

C. I want my writing to:

Encourage	Entertain	Inspire
Correct	Frustrate	Instruct
Teach	Convert	Direct
Challenge	Deepen	Equip
Comfort	Educate	Motivate

Look at the words you circled and the notes you jotted down. Turn these items into a declarative statement about who you are and what you want to accomplish by completing the following:

I view myself primarily as [answer from A]_____
and/or [answer from A], _____
who is primarily concerned about [answer from B], _____

_____

_____

and I want my writing to [answer from C]. _____

_____

Example:

I view myself primarily as a coach and encourager, who is primarily concerned about demystifying the writing process, and I want my writing to encourage my reader to take the next step in the process.

4

Write for Yourself

"Find a subject you care about and which you
in your heart feel others should care about."
—KURT VONNEGUT[1]

Whether you have *ambitions* to write or feel *called* to write or feel *pressure* to write, there's a lot to think about. My first piece of writing advice is to write for yourself. Not for an editor. Not for an audience. First and foremost, you have to write for you. But what in the world does that mean?

Writing for yourself means that you:

Write for the sake of writing.

If you want your writing to improve, you have to write. There is no other way to get better at writing than doing it. You must practice writing.

Someone will object, "Yes, but you may recall that I'm not actually all that interested in writing. It's something I have to do, not something I want to do with all my free time."

Please note that I am not asking you to write for the joy of writing. I'm saying that if you are going to become better at writing, you have to write without the promise of being published. You have to write without the promise of a platform. You have to write for yourself. If you want writing to become easier and more naturally a part of your life, you'll have to do it more frequently.

Think of time spent writing for yourself as time spent in a batting cage or at the driving range or practicing knife skills for cooking. It's a chance to master the fundamentals and develop muscle memory so that when you go play a game of baseball or a round of golf or cook dinner for guests, you enjoy the experience more fully—and have more confidence—because you're more comfortable with the basics. One reason people don't write is because getting started is hard. Getting started becomes easier and easier when you write regularly, for the sake of writing, without the promise of publication or the pressure of a deadline.

What does this look like practically? Some people set a goal to write every day for a certain amount of time or until they have drafted a certain number of words. I aim for thirty minutes per day or until I write five hundred words, whichever comes first. Usually, I run out of time before I run out of words. But writing every day, for myself, is making me better. It's helping me learn to overcome my greatest obstacle in writing: the empty page.

Your goal could be writing one morning per week. Or writing one blog post or newsletter per month. Whatever your goal, it shouldn't be to *publish* something right away, but simply to *make* something.

Writing for yourself means that you write for the sake of writing. It also means that you:

Write from the overflow of your knowledge, passion, and experience.

Most writers can't write about *everything*, although there are exceptions to this rule.

E. B. White, famous for *Charlotte's Web*, wrote essays about anything and everything: war, sports, chickens, the trees in New York City. And he did it well—all of it. But most writers are not E. B. White. Most writers can write well about a handful of things they truly know and care about. Truly great writing usually emerges from your passion, knowledge, and experience.

Kurt Vonnegut believed that writing about what you care about (writing for yourself) is ultimately what makes your writing appealing to others. "Find a subject you care about and which you in your heart feel others should care about," he advised. "It is this genuine caring, and not your games with language, which will be the most compelling and seductive element in your style."[2]

This is not novel information. But identifying what you really care about may take some self-reflection. When I first started writing, I wanted to be recognized as an "important" writer. (This temptation still lingers.) To be recognized as an important writer, I had to write about important things, and I had to write in a way that earned the approval of important people—scholars and "thought leaders" and such. The pressure to be important impacted both the subjects I wrote about and the style in which I wrote. You write *important* things in *serious* tones. Frankly, it sucked all the joy out of writing.

You may be immune to the temptation to be an important writer. But you face some kind of temptation. You may want to be recognized as a "successful" writer. Pursuing that goal might discourage you from writing about certain topics, such as failure. Or it may force you to tackle subjects about which you don't have any particular expertise—subjects like marriage or parenting or finances, because those are the kinds of books people seem to buy. You may be tempted to be known as a "popular" writer, and so you will be tempted to imitate the style and phrasing that are common of personalities on Facebook and Instagram.

When you identify the things you are knowledgeable about, passionate about, and have experience in, you are close to identifying your unique contribution. Lots of people may know what you know—many Christians read the same books and attend the same conferences. But no one has exactly the same experiences you have had. It's your unique combination of knowledge, passion, and experience that makes your perspective yours.

Think about the things you are passionate about, knowledgeable about, and have unique experience in—things people like to hear you talk about. You'll have an opportunity to do this in the next exercise (Find Your Focus Worksheet).

Finally, writing for yourself means:

Writing the kinds of things you enjoy reading.

If you don't enjoy reading how-to books about ministry, maybe you shouldn't *write* a how-to book about ministry. If you enjoy reading articles that provoke new ideas and experiences for you and avoid simplistic conclusions, you should consider writing articles that do those things too. If you don't enjoy reading graphic novels or listicles, don't aspire to write those things just because they are popular or attract attention.

Someone will object, "Yeah, but the market—"

And I'll interrupt. We're not talking about the market right now. We're talking about you.

But be prepared. Everyone doesn't enjoy reading what you like to read. And that means everyone won't enjoy reading what you like to *write*. Decide what kinds of things you want to write and be content with whatever audience you may find for that work.

Author Anne Lamott says this about publication:

Publication is not going to change your life or solve your problems. Publication will not make you more confident or more beautiful, and it will probably not make you any richer. There will be a very long buildup to publication day, and then the festivities will usually be over rather quickly.[3]

In light of this reality, it's important to find other reasons besides publication to motivate your writing. I say the first motive should be to write for yourself.

Do It: Find Your Focus Worksheet

Think about the things you are passionate about, knowledgeable about, and have unique experience in (what do people like to hear your perspective on?). Brainstorm items in each section of the focus worksheet at the end of the exercise. If a topic fits in one but not the others, put it in the one section. If it fits in all three, write it in all three.

Here's an example.

I'm passionate about organic gardening. However, I am not knowledgeable or experienced in it (unless you count killing lots of plants as "experience"), and no one really cares to hear me talk about it. For me,

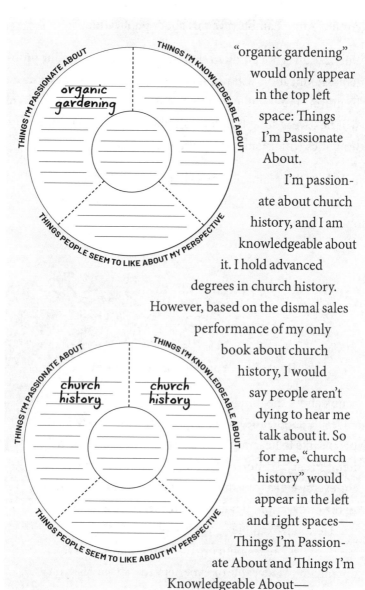

"organic gardening" would only appear in the top left space: Things I'm Passionate About.

I'm passionate about church history, and I am knowledgeable about it. I hold advanced degrees in church history. However, based on the dismal sales performance of my only book about church history, I would say people aren't dying to hear me talk about it. So for me, "church history" would appear in the left and right spaces— Things I'm Passionate About and Things I'm Knowledgeable About— but not the bottom third, Things People Seem to Like About My Perspective.

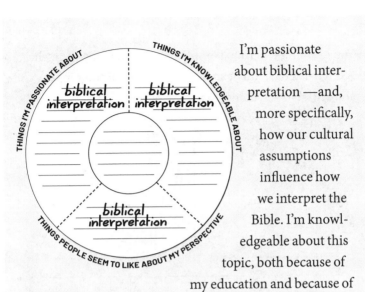

I'm passionate about biblical interpretation —and, more specifically, how our cultural assumptions influence how we interpret the Bible. I'm knowledgeable about this topic, both because of my education and because of my personal experience. And, lo and behold, this is a topic people actually seem to like to hear me talk (and write) about. So I might write "biblical interpretation" in all three spaces.

If something shows up in all three sections, rewrite it in the center circle. This may be a good topic (or topics, if there are more than one) for you to consider as your unique contribution.

Be as specific as you can. I'm not passionate and knowledgeable about biblical interpretation *in general*. I'm passionate and knowledgeable *in particular* about the ways our cultural conditioning affects the way we read and apply the Bible.

So I recommend this exercise to you—and I recommend that you be as thorough and specific as you can be.

You may find it hard to complete this exercise by yourself. Ask a trusted friend or spouse or mentor for their input and see what you come up with together.

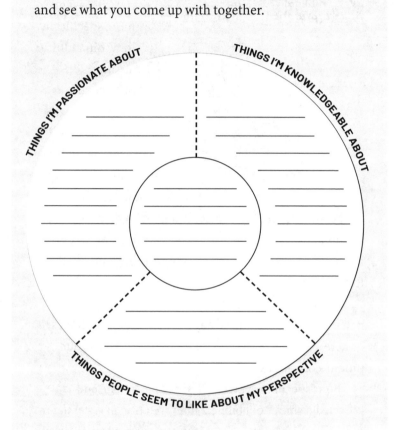

5

Never Write Only for Yourself

"If you write for God you will reach many men and bring them joy.
If you write for men—you may make some money and you may give someone
a little joy and you may make a noise in the world, for a little while.
If you write only for yourself you can read what you yourself have written and
after ten minutes you will be so disgusted you will wish that you were dead."

—THOMAS MERTON[1]

Learning to write for yourself will help you develop habits to keep writing, even if no one is reading what you write. And examining your areas of knowledge, passion, and experience will help you decide what you should write about.

At some point, though, you have to think about your reader. Especially if writing is your means of ministry, or an extension of your ministry, you have to be mindful of those to whom you are ministering. You have to decide how to engage your reader in a way that is clear and compelling.

Which is all to say that you have to write for yourself. But you cannot write *only* for yourself. You have to write for yourself in a way that serves your reader.

The third category in the Find Your Focus exercise is a step toward thinking about your reader. When you ask what people respond to most when you speak, teach, or write, you will discover something important about your unique contribution. But you are also at the beginning of learning something important about your readers: what stirs them and encourages them, what they're hungry for.

The Ideal Reader

There's a saying I frequently attribute to Flannery O'Connor, although I can't find anywhere that she actually said it. (It certainly feels like something she *would* say.) The possibly fictitious quotation goes like this: "The problem with most novels is that they are written for the 'average American boy,' but there is no such thing as the 'average American boy.'"

The point this (possibly apocryphal) quotation is trying to make is that writers often try to appeal to a broad audience, which is understandable. But in doing so, they aim their writing at a *generic* audience. The "average" Christian or the "typical" housewife. The thing is, there is no "average" or "typical" person, strictly speaking. There are only lots of individuals with unique experiences and circumstances. Your writing will be much better if instead of writing for the "average American boy," you decide to write for a "particular American boy." Maybe even one you know personally.

To do this well you have to have a clear idea who your reader is. In fact, you have to *choose* a reader and write with that person constantly in mind. Stephen King advises writers to have one person in mind as an audience when they write. He calls this person the "Ideal Reader," and his Ideal Reader is his wife, Tabby.

> When I write a scene that strikes me as funny . . . I am also imagining my [Ideal Reader] finding it funny. . . . During the actual

writing . . . the thought of making her laugh—or cry—is in the back of my mind. During the rewrite . . . the question—*is it funny enough yet? scary enough?*—is right up front. I try to watch her when she gets to a particular scene, hoping for at least a smile or—jackpot, baby!—that big belly-laugh with the hands up, waving in the air.[2]

The Ideal Reader becomes the filter for all your writing decisions. How do you know whether you should keep or delete a funny story in your essay? It won't make everyone laugh. Will it make your Ideal Reader laugh? If so, keep it. If not, delete it. How do you know if you included too much explanation (or too little) about a particular topic? If your Ideal Reader would be bored by the level of detail in the discussion, revise it. If they would need more explanation, explain some more.

Naming Your Reader

To know what your reader will find funny or what level of technical detail they will appreciate requires that you know him or her intimately. One way to accomplish this is to write to an actual person, as King does for Tabby. Anne Lamott wrote two books "that began as presents to people I loved who were going to die."[3] One was for her father after he was diagnosed with cancer. "I found myself desperate for books that talked about cancer in a way that would both illuminate the experience and make me laugh," she explains.[4] So she wrote stories about her family's experience with cancer and shared them with her dad as a gift. It's worth noting that in doing this, Lamott also wrote for herself. She wrote a funny book about cancer (the kind of book she wanted to read). She wrote a second book under similar circumstances. In both cases Lamott's intense focus on a tiny audience affected how she wrote.

"I wrote for an audience of two whom I loved and respected, who loved and respected me," she explains. "So I wrote for them as carefully and soulfully as I could—which is, needless to say, how I wish I could write all the time."[5]

Writing for a readership of one actual person is great. More often, though, your reader will be representative of a group you know well, such as the members of your congregation or the donors who support your organization. Your reader may be a composite person; someone you invent based on people you know well.

Some writers create composite readers in great detail, giving them names, birthdays, spouses and children, or even pets. There's a reason for this. Even if you don't go so far as to name your reader, you do need to know a lot about him or her—their level of education, professional experience, and basic cultural assumptions. You need to know what they *don't* know.

Have they been to seminary or Bible school? Do they know their denomination's creeds or statements of faith? You need to know what they fear, what motivates them, what they aspire to or dream of. Are they people of faith? People with questions? People with trauma? What obstacles stand between them and their goals? What would you tell them in your office or over a cup of coffee if they asked you for guidance about an aspect of their ministry or personal life?

Taking the time to identify your reader is beneficial even if you already have an established audience in your ministry or organization. All organizations have multiple audiences: staff, donors and other partners, the people you serve. Which of these readers do you have primarily in mind? If you've been preaching to the same congregation for a decade, your reader's needs and daily challenges have changed in the last ten years. If most of them were young adults then, they may be parents of young children now. Similarly, college students today are the same age as college students a decade ago. But they live in a different world. You'll need to adjust your writing accordingly so you aren't writing for a reader who no longer exists.

Who are you writing for ultimately, and what do you want to do for them?

If you know the answers to questions like these and are addressing the pressing needs of your reader, you have already achieved a true measure of success as a writer.

———————————•———————————

Do It: Identify Your Ideal Reader

Answering the questions below will help you identify *your* Ideal Reader.

Describe your Ideal Reader in general terms.
What cultural factors influence how they understand the world (age, location, gender, personality)?

_____

_____

_____

_____

How does your Ideal Reader get his or her information?
What sites do they visit? What authors do they read? What news outlets do they watch?

_____

_____

_____

_____

What is your Ideal Reader's greatest fear? What is their greatest aspiration?

_____

_____

What keeps your Ideal Reader from accomplishing his (or her) goals?

_____

_____

What kind of writing will your Ideal Reader find most helpful?

_____

_____

Take all this information and write it in paragraph form. Name your Ideal Reader, if you like. Share your Ideal Reader profile with your colleagues.

_____

_____

_____

_____

_____

_____

_____

_____

_____

_____

_____

_____

6

·

Avoid Alienating Everyone Else

Here's a lesson I learned the hard way: readers and writers are not always on the same page.

The first piece I wrote for public consumption was a blog review of a book that argued that it is "unmovable, historical fact" that most practices of contemporary churches were adopted from pagan culture and at odds with New Testament teaching. Thus "the church in its contemporary, institutional form has neither a biblical nor a historical right to function as it does."[1]

I was brand new to publishing, had just enough church history education to be dangerous, and was eager for a chance to flex my intellectual muscles. Also, I made one massive assumption: the readers of the blog were pastor types. So, surely, they would be as resistant as I am to the notion that the pastorate is pagan.

Boy, did I misread the room.

With the confidence that everyone on the internet was sure to agree with me, I wrote a snarky and uncharitable review. The comments starting piling up immediately. Readers were divided, but way more of them agreed with the book than I expected, and they called me out for my condescending response.

My point is, I wrote about the book (for a general audience) the way I would have talked about the book with a few close friends who I knew agreed with me. And who knew where I was coming from. And who shared my assumptions about history and ecclesiology and so forth. I made the mistake of assuming that my pastor-type audience and I shared certain presuppositions. I didn't have a particular reader in mind. I assumed the wrong posture. I misjudged my contribution. I assumed things I shouldn't have about my reader.

On the bright side, we got a lot of clicks.

Your writing decisions should be based on your interests and goals and your commitment to your reader. Remember, though, that others are reading too. And while you may not be able to please everyone, you can take steps to avoid offending everyone. If you are accustomed to communicating in an intimate environment where everyone knows you well, such as a church or classroom, the transition to writing for a broader audience can be bumpy.

Here are a few things to keep in mind:

Sarcastic humor may work live (often it doesn't), but it rarely communicates well in print.

This is a problem for me (as sarcasm is one of my spiritual gifts). I've edited pastors who mentioned their spouses in ways that were intended to be funny (i.e., "Obviously, I'm the brains of the relationship" or "Clearly, I'm the good looking one") but that doesn't come across right in print.

Jokes about theological positions or denominations or political groups with which you disagree are dangerous.

Even if you're a theological or denominational insider, you have to be careful making offhand remarks, especially in the current polarized climate of public discourse. If people have to read your bio to know you're a Baptist, for example, you should avoid taking potshots at Baptists. You should probably always avoid taking potshots at Baptists and everyone else, for that matter. The point is, there's a wink-and-nudge way of communicating with insiders that can get you into trouble when your work is in broader circulation. It doesn't really matter what you meant. What matters is how it sounds. Be gracious to a fault.

What is considered appropriate or acceptable, even among Christians, varies from region to region.

Everything from language (what's considered profanity) to imagery, metaphors, and tone will connect with some audiences and grate others, based on where they're from. What is clear and appropriate in your immediate context may not be either when your writing is read elsewhere. Lack of awareness of our own cultural context is one reason for frequent squabbles on social media. The internet brings people from different regions together in one place and makes it hard to establish context.

Education level, class/status, and other cultural differences can sneak through in illustrations and vocabulary.

If you rely heavily on illustrations about the frustrations of flying first class or the cost of private school tuition, you're going to lose people. I once heard a pastor tell a long story at a conference about doing his own stunts in a TV show. It was entertaining at first but ultimately a bit alienating for all us "normal people" in the audience who couldn't relate.

Remember, part of what you have to do is write for yourself. So I'm not asking you to fake it and make up illustrations that *you* don't resonate with just to connect with a reader. But it will be help-ful to anticipate who might be put off by your metaphors, illustra-tions, vocabulary, or style. Where you can avoid alienating people, try to do so. Where you can't, you at least won't be surprised by the pushback or criticism you receive.

One way to avoid missteps with your assumptions is to lay all your cards on the table in your writing. When I've written about issues related to race and ethnicity, for example, I've tried to clarify that I'm speaking not as a legal expert or a political commentator nor with any expertise in race relations but as a father and white male wrestling with my own baggage. On the whole, I think those caveats make readers more sympathetic to my reflections.

Tough skin is a topic for another day. But your readers will let you know when you're not on the same page. Try to take criticism graciously, and you'll learn to intuit what your readers are bringing to the table.

Do It: Anticipate Pushback

You identified your target audience in the Ideal Reader exercise. This exercise will help you anticipate the audi-ence(s) that may be harder or less natural for you to con-nect with. Choosing to target *one* audience means choos-ing to disappoint another audience. That's ok. Just want you to be prepared.

Look at your Ideal Reader profile and your personal profile. Answer the following questions:

1. What groups or types of readers might be hardest for you to connect with?

_____

_____

_____

2. What groups will be most likely to disagree with or mis-understand you in these areas:

Theological or doctrinal commitments

_____

_____

_____

Social or political opinions

_____

_____

_____

Cultural perspective

_____

_____

_____

Personal experience

_____

_____

_____

Other?

_____

_____

_____

3. Review your answers. Which of these issues can you address in your work by making small adjustments or additions, without compromising your personal vision or abandoning your Ideal Reader?

_____

_____

_____

_____

_____

_____

_____

4. Review your answers. About which of these issues will you simply have to accept disagreement?

_____

_____

_____

_____

_____

7

•

A Million Experts and Counting

My first full-time teaching position resulted in my teaching a course (Survey of the Bible) in the very same classroom in which I *took* the course as a student exactly fifteen years before. I mentioned this to my students (who were less interested in this tidbit than I was) and then proceeded to teach about Genesis 1.

The strangest thing happened.

They started taking notes. I said things about the Bible. They believed the things that I said were true and wrote them down in their notebooks.

Part of me recognized that this was the moment I'd been working toward for years. Three degrees, lots of loans and microwave ramen, and years of papers and exams all in the service of this one moment. I wanted to teach and now I was teaching.

At the same time, another part of me wanted to stop everything and say, "Hang on a second. I'm still sorting some things out. Intelligent, godly people disagree about these things. I could be wrong!"

I was drawn to teaching because it is consequential. It makes a difference. But somehow, never before that moment had I paused to weigh the enormous responsibility of saying important things to young learners who will assume that I know what I'm talking about. It was hard to believe these students would apply those things in their lives and *live differently* because of something I said.

What's true here of teaching is true also of writing. Writing matters. It makes a difference. It shapes and changes lives. And, for all these reasons, we can and should be excited about the prospect of sharing our ideas through writing and expanding our ministry through the written word. At the same time, we should also be sober-minded about the responsibility that comes with that awesome possibility.

For all these reasons and because writing is telepathy, basically, and a deeply personal and potentially vulnerable human transaction, Stephen King says,

> You can approach the act of writing with nervousness, excitement, hopefulness, or even despair . . . You can come to the act with your fists clenched and your eyes narrowed . . . You can come to it because you want a girl to marry you or because you want to change the world. Come to it any way but *lightly*.[1]

Why not come to writing lightly? Because the people who choose to be your readers have paid you an extraordinary honor. They have given you their attention for the length of time it takes them to read your post or book or newsletter. They have given you some measure of authority to shape the way they understand the world and how to live their lives. You honor their investment in you when you take your task seriously.

E. B. White told an interviewer for the *Paris Review*,

> I do feel a responsibility to society because of going into print: a writer has the duty to be good, not lousy; true, not false; lively,

not dull; accurate, not full of error. He should tend to lift people up, not lower them down. Writers do not merely reflect and interpret life, they form and shape life.[2]

If this is true of writing *in general*, then surely it is even more true of writing about matters of faith for people of faith. You may be totally confident that your position on a subject is the right one, and you feel that your ministry of writing is to set everyone straight. You might be entirely unsure that your position is the right one, and you feel that your ministry of writing is a way to sort it out. Fine. Either way the fact that your ideas appeared on a blog or in a magazine or book will establish you as an authority on the subject in the minds of many readers. "He must know what he's talking about," someone will say. "I mean, he wrote a book about it." One way we summarize someone's qualifications to speak authoritatively on a topic is to say, "He basically wrote the book on the issue."

The point is, writing is consequential. You may approach writing any number of ways: playfully, humorously, soberly. But don't approach it *casually*.

Here's a short survey of terrifying Bible verses I've paraphrased that address the danger of taking lightly the job of teaching about consequential matters:

Are you a teacher in Israel and you don't understand? (John 3:10)

Whoever presumes to be a teacher will be judged more severely. (James 3:1)

Better to be drowned than to lead someone astray. (Matt. 18:6)

In most places in the Bible, God's severest judgment is reserved not for the "average" Israelite who follows a wayward teacher, but for the prophet, priest, or teacher who assumes power, privilege, and platform. Setting ourselves up as guardians of the faith puts us in a position of great responsibility and accountability.

You may well be called to expand your ministry by defending doctrine, calling people to greater faithfulness, etc. I'm not questioning your calling or motives. Just accept this as a gentle reminder that such a calling should not be accepted lightly.

Nearly a million books are published every year in America. That's a million people per year who think they have something meaningful to say. Maybe they do. But before you join their number, it's a good idea to check yourself.

PART 2

The Process

8

•

Make a Plan

In previous sections you began thinking in broad terms about what topics you ought to address in your writing. You should write about topics that you are passionate about, that you know something about, and that people want to hear your opinion about. Identifying those handful of topics is an important first step in understanding who you are as a writer. This chapter is designed to help you get even more specific.

You also started thinking about your target audience. You won't stop thinking about those things. Your vision will sharpen with experience. But it's time now to give greater attention to narrowing your major topic areas into specific topics.

You may have determined in the previous exercises, for example, that you should write about preaching or community development or adoption. Great. The problem is, each of those topics is *enormous*. If you're planning to write a short piece, like a blog post or article, you can't possibly talk about everything related to preaching or community development or adoption. Even if you plan to write a book on the topic, you still can't possibly cover everything. You're going to have to be selective.

But how do you decide what to include and what to leave out? And where do you start?

The first step in the writing process is **planning**. We'll identify three phases or elements of the planning process.

The first is *brainstorming*.

The second is *researching*.

The third is *outlining*.

The purpose of these three phases is to help you narrow your subject matter from a broad topic down to a focus that's specific enough for you to address within the limits (pages, words, or time) of your writing project.

If it helps to think about writing in terms of the cooking metaphor I introduced in chapter one, the phases of the planning stage might function like this:

- Brainstorming is saying, "I'm in the mood for Mexican food. What are my options?"

- Researching is thumbing through recipe books for inspiration.

- Outlining is deciding what dish you're going to cook and what groceries you need to buy to cook it.

At the end of this process, you're a still a long way from eating dinner. But you've made progress. There's no meal without a plan.

The exercises will guide you deeper into each of these elements. Let's start with a brief overview.

The goal of the first element of the planning stage—**brainstorming**—is to determine the range of subtopics you could possibly write about related to your general subject. This phase is a bit like cleaning out a closet—the mess gets bigger before it gets smaller.

The idea is to get your head around the enormity of a topic and then choose what smaller part of it you want to focus on. There's a step in Part 2 that includes an example and some suggestions.

The next element in the planning stage is **researching**. I don't mean "research" in the academic sense—although that may be appropriate for some projects. In this context, by "research" I simply mean becoming familiar with the conversation that's already going on about the topic you're writing about.

Research helps you identify what parts of your subject matter have been sufficiently addressed and where there are still gaps. Research can free you from the pressure of trying to say *everything* and help you identify where you can make a unique contribution. Your research will be further informed by how you understand your unique contribution and your reader. There are tips for research in chapter 10.

The final element of the planning stage is **outlining**. The purpose of outlining is to chart a path before you start writing. You can deviate from the path as you go. But most people find it helpful to have an idea of where they're headed. There are tips for outlining in chapter 11.

It's a whole lot easier to put words on a blank page if you've taken some time first to brainstorm, research, and outline. If you complete the planning exercises, you'll be better equipped to plan out future writing projects.

9

•

Brainstorm

In a previous exercise (Find Your Focus worksheet), you began listing topics that are of interest to you and that you have some experience or knowledge of. It's possible that at this point there are two or three topics that all seem equally interesting to you, and you don't know how to choose between them. It's also possible that you know exactly what topic you want to write about, but you don't know how to write about the topic effectively.

A helpful first step is brainstorming. I recommend that you complete a brainstorming exercise for as many topics as you are contemplating writing about. For example, if three topics are equally interesting to you at this point, complete a brainstorming exercise for all three of them. The process of brainstorming can help you decide which of your options to choose.

There are many good ways to brainstorm. Here are two.

Mind mapping

The goal here is to get a comprehensive view of a topic, including all the subtopics and issues you *could* write about. Say you want to write about your experience adopting children. First, you'd write the big topic in the middle of a page:

Then you'd start thinking about all issues related to adoption. For example, there are different kinds of adoption:

Then things get more complicated:

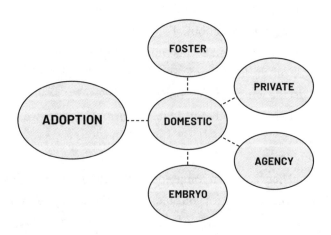

Keep building out your topic until you get everything on the page.

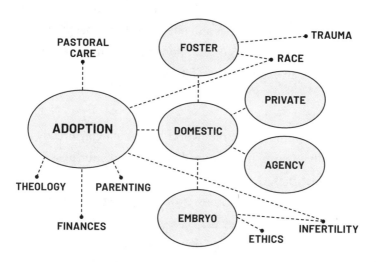

If the sight of this sprawling web of ideas has you reaching for the Xanax, don't despair. The goal of this exercise is not to overwhelm you or stun you into silence; it's to help you find your contribution. You won't have the final word on *all* of this. (You probably won't have the final word on *any* of this.) But you will have something valuable to say about *some* of it that will be of great benefit to *someone*.

Look at your mind map and identify the subtopics you want to address. When you start brainstorming, you'll likely find that you won't write about the topic in the big bubble in the middle. You'll write about one of the smaller, more specific "nodes." I might write about my experience as a white father raising brown children who were adopted as infants. We live in New York City, but we used to live in a small town in the South. I'm *not* writing about the history of adoption, the ethics of adoption, the theology of adoption, etc. (At least not directly.) Now I've bitten off something I can chew.

Once I've narrowed down my specific area of emphasis, I can broaden it out again. I can tell the story of my wife and me *before* the adoption. I can tell stories and offer reflections that touch on the history, theology, or ethics of adoption, but I am liberated from the pressure to be an expert in any of it. Make sense?

Sticky Notes

Mind mapping sometimes works best when you already know or can easily identify the relationships between your possible subtopics. Sometimes, though, there are just a lot of random thoughts in your head and you don't know how they fit together. When that's the case, you can use sticky notes (or note cards) to brainstorm.

Set aside some time—you may want to set a timer—and write your ideas on sticky notes (one idea per note) until the timer stops. Don't worry about the order in which you are writing them down. Just write. The goal is to get ideas on notes.

Let's revisit our previous topic of adoption as an example of how the sticky note exercise may work. You'd set the timer and write down everything that comes to mind, one item per note:

Issues in trans-racial adoption

What was adoption like in biblical times?

Paying for adoption

Supporting adoptive parents

Supporting birth moms

What does the Bible say about infertility?

Supporting adoptees

When your time is up or you've run out of ideas, sort through the notes and organize them. You may find that all of your notes fit together under a few broader categories. For example:

Adoption in
the Bible

Ethical and
Practical
Challenges

What was
adoption like
in biblical
times?

Issues in
trans-racial
adoption

What does the
Bible say about
infertility?

Paying for
adoption

Pastoral
Care Issues

Once you've completed this exercise, you may discover that you have elements of a story that you can now arrange sequentially or chronologically. You may find it helpful to brainstorm again, this time with the mind mapping exercise, using the categories you generated on the sticky notes.

Supporting
adoptees

However you do it, find a way to get your big ideas down where you can assess them and narrow them into a manageable project.

Supporting
birth moms

Supporting
adoptive
parents

10

How to Research for Writing

Imagine you walk into a room where people are seated around a table, embroiled in hearty discussion about some important topic. How would you go about joining that conversation in a way that's helpful for you and everyone else?

There are right ways and wrong ways. One wrong way would be to pull a chair up to the table and start sharing your opinion right away. Do that and someone may stop you to say, "Yes, I just said that exact thing. You would know that if only you had been listening."

Someone else might say, "That's a bit off the point. We were *actually* discussing something a little different."

A better approach would be to sit quietly and listen for a little while before making your own contribution. Make sure you understand the broader context of the conversation. Ask a few clarifying questions. Then, when the time is right, offer your opinion about the subject at hand.

I find it helpful to think of writing as joining an ongoing conversation. People were writing about your topic before you started writing about it, and people will still be writing about it after you finish. Your contribution will be most helpful if it takes the broader context—the ongoing conversation—into consideration.

Thinking about writing this way—as contributing to an ongoing conversation—has implications for your contribution, but also serves your audience. Some writers approach important questions as if they were the first person to pose them. One of the ways you serve your reader is by helping them connect their own questions to the ongoing conversation about that topic. You are the friend making introductions. Many of the million books published per year wouldn't need to be published if authors were committed to *not* repeating a conversation that had already begun.

Becoming familiar with the ongoing conversation about a topic requires research. Here are a few suggestions for getting started.

1. Get started with personal reflection.

Consider beginning your research with a session of focused self-reflection. Set a timer for thirty minutes and use the entire time to write whatever comes to mind.

The goal of this exercise is to help you find out what you already know, verbalize your most pressing questions, and identify the gaps in your understanding. Don't feel pressure to write in complete sentences. Jot down short phrases or incomplete sentences as you think of them. You'll have time to further organize these thoughts when you complete a first draft later.

Ideally this session of personal reflection will build on your previous brainstorming activity. Use the items from your brainstorming as prompts. On the mind map, the items are connected by lines. If you worked with sticky notes or notecards, the items are connected in columns. Explore the relationships between these items by articulating their relationship on paper.

How are they connected? What are the main points of conflict or tension, from your point of view? Which items do you find most compelling, discouraging, important?

Sometimes I complete this exercise in the first person, as a letter addressed to myself. I might write: "I'm interested in writing about the relationship between faith and mental health. I don't have any formal experience in studying mental health, but I have several close friends who are deeply devout and struggle with anxiety or depression and have expressed to me that these issues pose a challenge to their faith . . ." And so on.

Sometimes in the process of focused reflection, I'll stumble into a way forward—an interesting question, motivation, or new perspective on the project. At minimum, it helps me get words on a page that can be used for a rough draft later.

In my opinion, this stage of the process—personal reflection—should remain personal . . . and private. This isn't necessarily the time to broadcast your free-association thought experiment on your personal blog or social media feed. Keep it to yourself until you *really* know what you think.

2. Identify the key issues and questions.

After you spend time in self-reflection, you're ready to begin initial research. Search online for the shortest survey you can find on your topic: an article, a website, or even a Wikipedia page. Schedule a trip to your local library and look in the reference materials for encyclopedia articles. The tables of contents in college textbooks can help you get a big-picture view of many topics. If you aren't sure how to find a survey, try an internet search such as "an overview of faith and mental health" or "an introduction to faith and mental health." Ask a librarian for direction. A good, short survey can provide an essential overview (the main turning points in a history, for example, or the primary contested issues related to a current event).

Next, find two more short overviews for comparison. The first survey you read may quote other sources. Find those if you can, and read them too. A total of three or four short sources is often enough to give a good sense of the general conversation about a topic. They won't tell you everything you need to know, but they will help you identify what is common knowledge or general consensus on your topic and what areas are still contested or unaddressed.

Here's why this is important. When I worked for a magazine for ministry leaders, we regularly received submissions from pastors who wanted to write an article on the same subject: burn out. It's an important topic, to be sure. The problem was, all the proposals sounded the same. Invariably the author had experienced burnout himself. He spoke to other pastors and realized that lots of pastors had experienced burnout. Now he wanted to write an article about the dangers of burnout and some tips for how to avoid it.

We rejected most of these proposed articles, not because the topic wasn't important but because few writers took the time to research existing resources on ministry burnout. Because they didn't know what other articles (or books) had been written on the subject, they didn't have anything new to contribute to the conversation. A little bit of research could have strengthened their proposals —or convinced them that they didn't have anything new to offer at the proverbial table.

The key issues and questions you might write about are the things that aren't mentioned in the surveys and fail to receive attention in other resources. They are the items you take note of after you've done a little research and are left thinking, *But what about . . . ?* or *That doesn't explain . . .* or *My experience was quite different, for the following reasons . . . .* To return to our example of faith and mental health, what is it that no one seems to be writing about, the questions no one seems to be asking? You know they're important because you've experienced them or love someone who has. Dig deeper into those questions.

This is where your experience and the needs of your reader can help you determine what's important. If your readership is women in ministry, you might explore the issues related to faith and mental health that are particularly acute for women in ministry. If you experience anxiety and lead an organization, you might explore the relationship between anxiety and leadership.

3. Research the relevant questions and issues.

Once you know what issues and questions are central for you and your reader, you can focus additional research on those items. This process can snowball. One children's book describes the work of scientists, and it applies to writing:

> Ada Marie did what scientists do:
> She asked a small question, and then she asked two.
> And each of those led her to three questions more,
> and some of those questions resulted in four.[1]

It might be helpful to see how your issues and questions are addressed in related fields. For example, if you are specifically concerned about mental health issues for Christian women in ministry, consider researching mental health issues for women in leadership in general to gain perspective. Your unique contribution, the work that will most serve your reader, may be making the connection between these two slightly different fields of study.

4. Revisit your personal reflection.

There are multiple right ways to process what you learn. You might find it helpful to take the notes and insights you develop during research and compare them with your personal reflection. Incorporate what you learned in the process of researching into your reflection notes. Review your reflection and see which of your initial questions were answered. Which were unanswered? What surprises you about the answers? Your research may help you organize your thoughts into an outline, the subject of the next chapter. The process of outlining may help you see where you need to dedicate time to additional research. This way your research is always contributing to your first draft.

The amount of time you need for research will vary depending on how familiar you are with the current conversation on your topic and the length of your writing project. If, for example, you're writing a short piece (under 1,000 words), you may learn everything you need to know in a couple hours. If you're writing a book, you will need to dedicate considerably more time to research. If all of this sounds like a lot of work, take heart: it is.

But anything worth doing is worth doing right. Besides, the hard work you do at this stage will pay off for all future projects. "Good writers," says Roy Peter Clark, "fill up a reservoir of knowledge they can drain at a moment's notice."[2] Today it's a slog, but tomorrow you are writing from the overflow of your preparation. And, what is perhaps most important, doing your homework is one way to ensure that you do not come to the work of writing lightly.

11

•

Outline

Two kinds of outlines are useful for writing. The first, the *preliminary* outline, is the most common. The other kind of outline is less common—though maybe more *useful*—and we'll talk about it in a future chapter about revising our work.

The preliminary outline is useful *after* you've done some journaling, note-taking, and research and *before* you start writing a rough draft in earnest. It helps you organize your thoughts and keeps you focused as you write. It is *not* intended to limit the shape of the final project, unless, of course, you are writing for publication and have strict parameters within which you are expected to work. In all other cases, you may find as you start writing that you will need to deviate from your preliminary outline. That's no problem. The outline isn't a mandate; it's a suggestion.

The preliminary outline is the type most of us learned in grade school. It consists of a series of points and subpoints:

1. Introduction
2. Main Point 1
   a. Subpoint
   b. Subpoint

3. Main Point 2
    a. Subpoint
    b. Subpoint
    c. Subpoint
4. Main Point 3
    a. Subpoint
    b. Subpoint
5. Conclusion

So far this may be entirely familiar. This is step one. Step two gives us helpful guidelines for making important decisions.

After you've drafted an outline, like the one above, assign word count or page count limits to each point and subpoint. To be able to do this, you'll need to know a maximum total length for the entire project. Let's say for the sake of illustration that we're writing a 1,500-word blog post.

As a rule of thumb, plan for the introduction and conclusion to each be no more than 10 percent of the total length of the piece:

1. Introduction (150 words)
2. Main Point 1
    a. Subpoint
    b. Subpoint
3. Main Point 2
    a. Subpoint
    b. Subpoint
    c. Subpoint
4. Main Point 3
    a. Subpoint
    b. Subpoint
5. Conclusion (150 words)

That leaves us 1,200 words to work with. That means each of our main points gets about 400 words each, if each main point is prioritized exactly equally (more on that below).

1. Introduction (150 words)
2. Main Point 1 (400 words)
   a. Subpoint
   b. Subpoint
3. Main Point 2 (400 words)
   a. Subpoint
   b. Subpoint
   c. Subpoint
4. Main Point 3 (400 words)
   a. Subpoint
   b. Subpoint
5. Conclusion (150 words)

Of course, there's no rule that says you have to dedicate the same number of words to every main point. Kurt Vonnegut gives eight pieces of advice in "How to Write with Style." The longest section, Say What You Mean to Say, is 250 words, give or take a few. The shortest section has only six words. His advice for that section: "Do not ramble." In another short section, his advice is "Have the guts to cut."[1] In both cases, the number of words was appropriate for the advice. This is all to say that the word count distribution in the outline above is simply for example.

At this point, you may be ready to start drafting. If so, that's great. Follow your outline.

It's also possible at this point that your outline can help you make decisions about what you want to prioritize in your writing. Let's say, for example, that Main Point 1 is "a brief history of preaching."

There's no way you'll cover that topic sufficiently in 400 words. So you have a choice to make. Do you want to cut it entirely? Do you want to give it more space in your outline by reducing the amount of space you dedicate to another point? Working within a word count means that if you write more about one point, you'll have to write less about another. These are the hard decisions a writer makes. Outlining can help you make them.

Again, you're not making any permanent decisions at this point. This is a *preliminary* outline. But your outline can help you both organize and simplify your thoughts before you start writing.

Do It: Take the Next Step

Part 2 has covered a lot of ground. Choose one or more of the exercises in this step to help you apply what you've learned.

Brainstorm

Set a timer for thirty minutes. Working until the timer goes off, brainstorm by creating a mind map, writing on note cards, or whatever method you prefer.

Research

Set aside at least an hour for research. First, write down everything you can without accessing other resources. *You can—and should!—access your brainstorming notes.* After you've written all you can without referencing other materials, take a moment to identify your key questions. Note: Key questions may be the questions you, the writer, are interested in. However, the key questions may also be determined by your reader and the topics they have requested (or required!) that you write about.

Now find a short survey resource on your topic. What new questions does this resource raise? What questions does it answer?

Find and review at least two more short resources on your topic. How do these resources affect how you might write about your topic?

Outline

Draft a preliminary outline for your project, including word count or page count limits for each section.

Do It: Write a Mission Statement for Your Work

Let's pause, catch our breath, and review.

If you have worked straight through this book from the beginning with a specific project in mind, you have:

- reflected on your motivations for writing

- drawn some conclusions about your unique contribution as a writer

- identified your reader and considered what audiences might not appreciate what you have to say

That's a lot. Well done. You've also:

- brainstormed ideas
- conducted some research
- drafted an outline

At this point you are ready to write a draft. You are more ready than most people will ever be. Before you start drafting in earnest, I recommend one final calibration: write a mission statement for your work. I'm recommending this now, and didn't sooner, because all the things you've accomplished above have sharpened your vision. You are in a better position to articulate the purpose of your project.

Mark Bowden, author of *Black Hawk Down*, describes his goals as writer in this way:

> When I began working on this project in 1996, my goal was simply to write a dramatic account of the battle. . . . My contribution would be to capture in words the experience of combat through the eyes and emotions of the soldiers involved, blending their urgent, human perspective with a military and political overview of their predicament.[2]

> I wanted to combine the authority of a historical narrative with the emotion of the memoir, and write a story that read like fiction but was true.[3]

Bowden says a lot in less than a hundred words. He describes the tone ("dramatic account") and perspective ("eyes and emotions of the soldiers involved") and content ("military and political overview") of the book. He describes its impact: authoritative, emotive, impossible to put down.

Imagine how many pages of notes Bowden must have worked from, notes of all different types: military documents, news reports, eyewitness accounts, and more. The only force powerful enough to bring cohesion to these sources is the writer's vision, captured in this mission statement. It helped him decide what to keep and what to cut. It helped him measure success for himself. It helped him keep the reader in view at all times.

Here's another example of a helpful mission statement, drafted by a church planter I worked with:

> For my article, I envision a personal essay, written in the first-person, structured around a narrative arc that explores my attempts to lead our church further into the culture. The objective would be to invite readers to consider the ideas, efforts and concrete examples of one church plant's efforts in cultural engagement and expressiveness. I would like readers to conclude the article feeling informed and inspired to attempt humble exercises of culture-making of their own.[4]

A mission statement should include some or all of the following:

- **form** (i.e., memoir, essays, dramatic nonfiction, etc.)
- **content** (i.e., biblical exposition, experience of loss or grief, etc.)

- **effect/impact** for readers (i.e., draw readers into the story, convince readers of a truth, encourage self-reflection)

- personal **goals** as a writer (i.e., tell good stories and trust them to communicate truths, complete my first novella, convert a sermon into an essay, etc.)

- primary **motivation** for writing (i.e., to finally share my story, to help readers in similar situations, etc.)

Take a few minutes to draft your mission statement below:

_____

_____

_____

_____

_____

_____

_____

_____

_____

_____

_____

_____

_____

_____

12

•

Your Best 30 Minutes

Comedians work hard to craft a "tight 5" or "tight 10" stand-up routine. It's a portable set of exactly five or ten minutes that is honed and revised until it is sure to get laughs anywhere. It's a carefully crafted, thoroughly rehearsed, crowd-pleasing few minutes that the comedian knows by heart. For the audience, the material may feel fresh and spontaneous. For the performer, it is the result of lots of experience and hard work.

If you teach, preach, consult, train, coach, or catechize regularly, especially if you are invited to speak to new audiences, then you probably have a portable presentation that has been tested, honed, and revised until it is pretty successful everywhere, the result of a lot of experience and hard work. You might think of this as your "tight 30" (or forty-five or sixty or whatever). I typically call it "your best thirty minutes."

A great way to get started writing, if getting started is the big challenge for you, is to begin by writing down your best thirty minutes. It's the presentation you give all the time, and you've got it down cold. It's the workshop you've led so many times that you can't understand why anyone finds it interesting because, for you, it's old news. It's the sermon people ask you to preach over and over. Sometimes they ask if you've written about it somewhere.

Your best thirty minutes may be:

- A sermon

- A guest lecture

- A professional presentation

- Advice on a particular topic

- A pep talk you give volunteers, new employees, etc.

Your best thirty minutes may currently exist in a number of formats other than print. It may be a recorded audio or video file, an outline or scribbled set of notes, a slide deck. That is, it may take a little work to get the contents onto paper. But you already have the material down by heart.

Here's an example from my work life. My colleague Dave coaches church planters around the world. He was trying to figure out how to scale up. He needed to do more than coach pastors; he needed to coach coaches to coach pastors. He knew that would require some sort of distributable resource—a pamphlet or book or online course—but he wasn't sure where to start.

I asked him: "When someone reaches out to you about coaching for the first time, how do you start the conversation?"

"We usually meet over coffee or Skype and I explain what coaching is and what it isn't, what they can expect from a coaching relationship—that sort of thing."

"Do you always cover the same material and answer the same questions?"

"More or less, sure."

That was his best thirty minutes. So I encouraged him to write it up.

Each standard question is a section or chapter. Answer the question the way you would answer it in person. The result was a sixty-or-so-page document that has now been distributed, translated, and adapted around the world. Dave can only be in one place at one time. But his best thirty minutes can be anywhere and everywhere at once.

Your best thirty minutes can be a finished product or it can be the beginning of a longer project (or both). Once you get it on paper, you might realize that to really benefit from your best thirty minutes, a reader needs some additional background information or context. Great. Write that next. Or maybe you realize that to really connect with a reader, your best thirty minutes needs additional application and illustration. Perfect. Write that next. Or you can share it with someone who can give feedback, ask clarifying questions, and offer suggestions.

Your best thirty minutes is a great place to start writing if you already speak or teach regularly. If you aren't sure what your best thirty minutes is, ask a friend, spouse, or colleague. They know.

13

•

Draft

Once you've decided what topic to write about and have made a plan, there's nothing left to do but write a first draft.

Remember, though, that writing is a three-stage process: planning, drafting, revising. We have entered stage *two*: drafting.

The goal in the drafting stage is to get words on a page. You are successful when you get words down—whether or not they are any good. They probably won't be good. The fact is, all first drafts are lousy.

Anne Lamott calls the first draft "the child's draft, where you let it all pour out and then let it romp all over the place, knowing that no one is going to see it and that you can shape it later."[1] It may seem inefficient to begin with a lousy first draft, and it just might be, except that there isn't any way around it. And besides, the way you get a great second draft is to start with a lousy first draft. Anne Lamott again:

> Just get it all down on paper, because there may be something great in those six crazy pages that you would never have gotten to by more rational, grown-up means. There may be something in the very last line of the very last paragraph on page six that

you just love, that is so beautiful or wild that you now know what you're supposed to be writing about, more or less, or in what direction you might go—but there was no way to get to this without first getting through the first five and a half pages.[2]

You will occasionally write a good first draft, but don't let that lone exception alter your worldview. It's best to assume that all the rest of the first drafts you will ever write will be lousy. And that's ok. You'll have a chance to make your first draft better in the next stage—revising. That's where the magic happens. In the drafting stage—I repeat—the goal is filling an empty page.

To return to our cooking metaphor: **planning** is like choosing a recipe and selecting ingredients. **Drafting** is chopping and measuring those ingredients. It gets the right ingredients on the counter. But it does not turn those ingredients into a meal you would serve your guests.

Every metaphor breaks down. Unlike following a recipe, when you start writing your first draft you may deviate from your outline. You may write way more on some sections than you expected and way less on others. That's ok. Don't worry about the final product. Just keep writing.

You'll be tempted to worry about any number of things while you write your first draft. You may worry about the final length of your project. You may be afraid, for example, that you don't have enough to say or that you have too much to say. You may worry about how the paragraphs are organized, whether they flow correctly and make a cogent argument or tell a compelling story. You may worry that you don't have a strong introduction or a clear conclusion. You'll worry about next year's taxes and the rising cost of a college education and the disappearance of honeybees. If you are worried about these things, you're in good company. But do your best to ignore those concerns and *just write.*

The little voice that brings those issues to your mind while you're writing is your inner editor speaking. Your inner editor has a valuable contribution to make in the writing process, but not at this stage. The inner editor works during the next stage, in **revising**. Right now, in the drafting stage, you need to figure out how to silence or ignore your inner editor. There's a saying attributed to Ernest Hemingway: "Write drunk. Edit sober." Whether or not he actually said it doesn't matter. It's good advice. The clear-minded, detail-oriented editor will have his or her say. But not now. Now is the time to "write drunk"—that is, to write unselfconsciously and with abandon.

You may have to experiment a little before you learn how to silence (or ignore) your inner editor. Over time I've learned, for example, that I self-edit much less when I:

- Write first thing in the morning. (It's as if my inner editor works best in the afternoon.)

- Write longhand with pen and paper (for some reason I'm much more tempted to self-edit when I type on a computer).

- Write for a set period of time. (I aim for thirty minutes a day.)

The big takeaway at this point is this:

This stage of the writing process is improved by practice.

This is where the discipline of writing regularly and the development of good writing habits really pay off. The more you practice, the better you'll get to know yourself and how you work best. The more you practice, the more comfortable you'll become with the process. All my first drafts are lousy—but I expect that at this point, and it doesn't worry me too much anymore.

The great reward of drafting is that it is a process of discovery. If you're like me, you'll discover what you really think about your topic *while* you're drafting. You may discover that the project you thought should be a book should actually be an article, or the other way around. You'll get your thoughts out of your head and onto paper where you can sort them and sharpen them.

You may be pleasantly surprised by what you find rattling around in your brain.

Do It: Drafting Tips and Tools

The goal of the drafting stage is to get words on the page. Do not be concerned about the length, quality, word choice, or content of your work. There are, in fact, only two rules for drafting:

1. Don't edit yourself.

2. Don't stop to compose or collect your thoughts. Just write.

You will break both of these rules. But keep them in mind just the same. If you aren't accustomed to writing, you will likely find it difficult to fill a blank page with words. You will write a sentence you don't like and you'll be tempted to erase it and rewrite it. Resist the temptation! Instead, just write another sentence that you like better (or maybe even less) than the last one. *But then I'll have two sentences that say exactly the same thing!* Yep. It's your inner editor's job to clean up that mess later. Your job now is just to write.

You will find it hard to resist the urge to self-edit. You may find it hard to think of *anything at all* once you sit down to write. The following tips and tools can help you maximize your drafting time.

Set a timer

The prospect of writing for an unlimited amount of time can be intimidating. Sometimes it helps to set a timer. (You may have noticed that many of the exercises in this book ask you to set a timer when you work.) Creating a time limit can force you to focus on the task at hand. To make the most of this time, eliminate all other distractions—phone notifications, emails, social media. If you're just starting out, set the timer for 15 minutes and work your way up to 30 minutes, then 45 minutes, then an hour. Setting a time provides an easy definition for writing success: you are successful when you write for the entire time.

Write a letter

Getting started is often the hardest part. Consider writing about your topic in the form of a letter to a friend, colleague, or even your younger self. What do you want your friend, colleague, or younger self to understand about your topic? What questions should they be asking? What intimidates you about writing about this topic? What excites you? At some point you will have to convert the format into whatever form you determined in your mission statement.

It's an extra step. But that's ok. Writing a first draft in a letter format can help you write naturally (in your normal voice) and personally. It also forces you to think about one reader.

Write by hand

Typing on a computer makes writing easier. But it also makes *editing* easier, and editing is the enemy of free writing. If you have a tendency to self-edit as you write, consider writing the old-fashioned way: on a piece of paper with pen or pencil. Additionally, writing by hand can be less frustrating for those whose typing fingers can't keep up with the flow of their thoughts. You may find that writing by hand gives you a greater sense of rhythm and rest as you write. There's also a lot of good research that suggests that writing things down helps you internalize and process the material better. That's helpful later when you revise.

Dictate, then transcribe

Some writers process verbally, which means traditional free writing exercises work against their strengths. If your ideas flow more naturally when you speak than when you write, try dictating into a recording device (a smartphone works fine) during your free writing session. When you're finished, you can use an online service to transcribe your audio file so you have text to work with in the next stage of the process. As with writing in a letter format, this approach adds a step to the process. But it's worth it if it helps you get your first draft down on paper.

14

•

A Good Day of Writing

Writing is as simple as putting just the right words in just the right order, again and again, until you're finished. The trouble is, most days all you can think of is the wrong words and they clearly are in the wrong order and you can't imagine you'll ever be finished. And that's the really demoralizing thing about writing. Writing isn't like hanging drywall or improving your golf swing or invading a country. There aren't always definable steps in the process by which the writer may measure his or her progress. Either you're "finished" or you're not.

Here are some metrics and milestones to keep you buoyed in the drafting process:

Sometimes a good day of writing . . . involves brainstorming, mind-mapping, outlining, or otherwise organizing your thoughts. Draft an outline. Jot down notes on a napkin. Think and doodle. You may not compose sentences or paragraphs. But this is real work.

Sometimes a good day of writing . . . involves getting some of these thoughts on a piece of paper. There's time later to worry about what order the words ought to go in. If you start with a blank white page and end the day with something—anything—on it, that's a victory.

Sometimes a good day of writing . . . results in clearly articulating a single important concept or thought. It's not glamorous, but the most important part of writing is often finally being able to say what you mean. Maybe it's the thesis you've been struggling to formulate, the payoff you've failed to make tangible, or the crucial connection you've been unable to articulate. If you finally pin one of these down, even if you walk away with only one good sentence, it's a good day. It's as important as getting the foundation of your new building square, plumb, and level.

Sometimes a good day of writing . . . is spent cleaning your desk. Or washing the car. Or mowing the lawn. Cal Newport, who is something of a productivity expert, calls these sorts of activities "productive meditation." "The goal," he writes, "is to take a period in which you're occupied physically but not mentally—walking, jogging, driving, showering—and focus your attention on a single well-defined professional problem."[1] The key here is focusing your attention while you do these things. Otherwise these are just avoidance behaviors. (If you're like me, you'll become very good at avoidance behaviors while you're trying to get better at writing.) Almost without fail, I do my best writing in my head while I'm doing something else. Then there follows a mad dash somewhere—to find a notebook or computer—to capture the words before they escape. The point is, sometimes a good day of writing doesn't involve any "writing."

Sometimes a good day of writing . . . includes reading good writing that helps you find your voice. There are days when I feel like I have plenty to say, but by the time I try to put words to paper, they feel stilted and unnatural. Often the solution is to just keep writing; you can revise tomorrow. Other times the solution is to read someone who helps you speak naturally. True confession: when I sing along with "More Than a Feeling," I feel like a rock star. When I read Flannery O'Connor or Kurt Vonnegut, I feel like a writer. Sometimes Sister Flannery (and others) give me the boost I need to speak for myself.

Finally, sometimes a good day of writing . . . results in quantifiable forward progress: you type actual words—words that you like and may well keep—into your document and save them. These are good days. But please do not confuse a day like this as a flash of inspiration. That's not it at all. What this is, instead, is the process working. It's the result of hard, consistent work, finally paying off. For me, these days usually follow several days like the ones described above: days spent doodling, turning out bad prose like beef through a meat grinder, slowly—slowly—pulling together clear, finely-tuned sentences here and there. Then there's a rush of productivity when things finally fall into place, and I might compose several pages in a sitting.

Those are the days I like best, of course. But I'm learning to consider the other days good days of writing. That way when someone asks me how the writing's going, I can say, "Great, thanks."

Do It: Write a Draft

Friends, the time has come to put pen to paper and begin drafting your blog/article/sermon/book. Here are a few things to keep in mind about your first draft:

First drafts are always bad. The purpose of the first draft is to get ideas out of your brain and onto paper. Once the ideas are on paper, we can refine them, reorganize them, and revise them. We do all that work in the second draft.

Write your first draft to "natural length." Don't worry at this point about word limits. Just write until you've said everything you want to say on your subject—or, at least, everything you've planned to in your outline. You will worry about length in the second draft.

Talk about your work. It might be helpful to set up a coffee meeting with a friend or colleague who is familiar with your topic. Collaboration is an important part of the process. Just remember to plan for these conversations so you don't run out of writing time.

Make a date. Which brings us to our last point: if you don't already have a deadline for your piece, create one. Lorne Michaels, creator of the television show Saturday Night Live (SNL), is credited by comedian Tina Fey with saying, "The show doesn't go on because it's ready; it goes on because it's 11:30."[2] Most of us don't have the hard deadline of a live broadcast, thank goodness. Even if it's self-imposed and arbitrary, a deadline can help you prioritize your writing.

There's nothing left to do now but write.

15

•

Revise

In one of my favorite essays of his, E. B. White laments the fact that "a writer does a lot of work the reader isn't conscious of, and never gets any credit." As a point of comparison, White offers the work of photographers, as photography was becoming more popular when White was writing in the early twentieth century. "The act of photography has been glorified in the newspicture magazines, and even in the newspapers," White notes. "In photography, the goal seems to be to prove beyond a doubt that the cameraman, in his great moment of creation, was either hanging by his heels from the rafters or was wedged under the floor with his lens at a knothole."[1]

The aim of the writer is quite the opposite. "The hope and aim of a word-handler is that he may communicate a thought or an impression to his reader without the reader's realizing he has been dragged through a series of hazardous or grotesque syntactical situations." To raise the public's interest in writing, White muses, maybe editors should include captions below the text in newspapers that celebrate the writer's otherwise invisible work. "This paragraph was exposed for eighteen minutes, in a semi-darkened room. The writer was leaning far out over his typewriter, thinking to beat the band."[2]

The final stage in the writing process is **revising**. Revising is not glamorous work. No one waxes poetic about great feats of revision. But I assure you, revising is where the real magic of writing happens. As William Zinsser puts it in *On Writing Well*, "rewriting is the essence of writing."[3]

Picking back up with our cooking metaphor:

Planning is choosing a recipe and selecting ingredients.

Drafting is chopping and measuring those ingredients—getting all the right elements in one place within arm's reach.

Revising is putting together all those ingredients, in the right proportions and the right order, to make a meal you're proud to share.

And, of course, that final stage of the process also involves spontaneity and discovery.

You may find in the process of revising, for example, an image or phrase or refrain that you can pull through the entire post or article or chapter you're writing to provide cohesion.

In the course of revising your draft, you will cut sentences and paragraphs and maybe even entire sections that seemed to fit when you wrote them and now seem to distract from your main point or hinder the flow of your argument. That's ok. You can use those deleted sections as raw material for another project.

During revision, you will reorganize the paragraphs you keep. You'll identify the lead (how you get the reader *into* your topic) and the conclusion (how you bring the reader to a satisfying end). You'll determine the final shape of the composition. You'll adjust the length of sentences, the pacing, and your vocabulary.

Obviously, your second draft will be quite different from your first draft. This is a good thing. This is the process working as the process should work. And it doesn't mean that your first draft was a failure. Remember: French fries start out as potatoes.

Remember this too: revising is one *stage* of the writing process. But that doesn't mean you will revise only once. It usually takes me several drafts—sometimes as many as six or seven—before I feel satisfied with my own writing. Somewhat ironically, it often takes that many drafts before my writing sounds natural. So be prepared. You may revise several times. You probably should.

Do It: Reverse Outlining

Earlier we talked about two kinds of outlining. The first is a preliminary outline, which most of us are familiar with. But it's the second kind of outline I find most helpful, and I use it all the time during the writing process when revising my own writing or editing someone else's.

Sometimes an article or chapter just doesn't flow right, or it hints at an important point but never gets around to saying it outright. Often when this is the case, I can *sense* it's the case, but I can't quite put my finger on what's wrong. When that happens, I reverse outline the problem passage— or even the entire blog post or chapter. Almost always, this process reveals where the breakdown is.

Here's how it works: I summarize every paragraph of my composition in one sentence each.

So, for example, this paragraph:

But imagination is not the opposite of reality or the enemy of truth. In fact, we do ourselves an enormous disservice when we ignore the imagination (whether intentionally or accidentally) and only develop the intellect. For the intellect is only half the equation. Imagination is the partner of the intellect. One is not more important than the other; they do different things. But because we have neglected the imagination, it deserves our special attention.[4]

Becomes this sentence:

The imagination partners with the intellect to communicate truth, so we need to pay attention to the imagination.

I do this with every paragraph in the section or chapter I'm trying to make sense of. Then I put the sentences together in an outline. For example:

Introduction

- Faith is an act of imagination, and a healthy imagination is crucial to the Christian life.

- Some disagree because the Christian faith is based on facts, and some believe imagination is antithetical to facts.

- The Christian tradition has been focused for generations on demonstrating the reasonability of faith.

- The imagination partners with the intellect to communicate truth, so we need to pay attention to the imagination.

When you try this with your own writing, don't trouble yourself with whether or not the summary sentences are good writing. The goal is to see if the thoughts develop logically from one paragraph to the next. If they do, then the outline will reflect this. If they don't, then the outline should show you where the problem is. Often the reverse outline reveals that two paragraphs make the same basic point and are therefore redundant. These paragraphs could be combined or one of them eliminated.

If the points flow logically but something is still amiss, it may be that what you need are stronger transitions between paragraphs. Reducing a paragraph to one sentence forces me to ask what a reader needs to know in order to follow me from point two to point three (for example).

Reverse outlining takes time. But this process will help you clarify your writing.

16

•

Delete Most of the Words

Clear writing is usually concise. The more words we use, the more likely we are to miscommunicate. Or to over explain something simple. Or to flat out say the wrong thing. That's why the Bible says, "When there are many words, transgression is unavoidable, but he who restrains his lips is wise" (Prov. 10:19).

Unfortunately, many of us are trained by reading bad writing to believe that writing clear and concise sentences is a sign of intellectual weakness. (Or some such nonsense.) This is especially true if you've spent much time in academic circles, where bad writing abounds. Academics often use five words where one or two will do.

Sometimes we are tempted to use too many words when we try to write in a conversational—or what William Strunk called "breezy"—style. Strunk gave this example:

> Well, guys, here I am again dishing the dirt about your disorderly classmates, after passing a weekend in the Big Apple trying to catch the Columbia hoops tilt and then a cab-ride from hell through the West Side casbah. And speaking of news, howzabout tossing a few primo items this way?[1]

In his commentary on this passage, Strunk points out that the writer has said exactly nothing and he's spent about fifty words doing it. "The breezy style is often the work of an egocentric, the person who imagines that everything that comes to mind is of general interest and that uninhibited prose creates high spirits and carries the day."[2] Times and idioms have changed, but this sort of writing is still with us today.

So for the sake of clarity and your own sanctification, I recommend you delete all the words you can. Most manuscripts easily could be reduced by 25 percent without sacrificing any crucial content. If that seems unlikely, you might be right. William Zinsser thought that most first drafts "can be cut by 50 percent without losing any information or losing the author's voice."[3] Of course you want to delete the right words. But that isn't hard to do.

Here are some tips with examples:

Simplify redundancies.

"In our minds, we thought . . ." is not a false statement. Our mind is where we do our thinking. But because our mind is the *only* place we do our thinking, the prepositional phrase "in our minds" is redundant. Just say, "We thought." No one will wonder if you did it with your toes. (Note: word count reduced by 60 percent.)

Beware of prepositional phrases.

Sometimes we'll be tempted to address an issue "in a broad manner" when we should simply address it "broadly." Prepositional phrases are bland. Why say someone arrived at his point "in a roundabout way" when you could say he made his way there "circuitously"? (Note: in both cases the word count is reduced by 75 percent.)

To appeal to Zinsser again:

Instead of "with the possible exception of" write "except."

Instead of "due to the fact that" write "because."

Instead of "he totally lacked the ability to" write "he couldn't."

Instead of "for the purpose of" write "for."[4]

Trust your verbs.

Don't use the noun (nominal) form of a word when there is a verb form: Instead of "provide a reorientation," say "reorient" (a 66 percent reduction). Instead of saying "There is no possibility for success," say "success is impossible" (a 50 percent reduction). Instead of "to be a deterrent," write "to deter" (another 50 percent reduction). Letting your verbs do the work keeps your prose clear and active.

Ruthlessly eliminate jargon (especially religious jargon)

If I were supreme dictator of Christianity, the first thing I'd do is outlaw a number of popular phrases from our collective vocabulary. This is a non-exhaustive list:

- pour into
- lean into
- love on
- marinate in
- do life with

These aren't awful things to say. But they are basically meaningless. "Love on" isn't different than "love," except that it's more awkward. And I would prefer that no one pour anything into me. My cup runneth over already, thank you very much. Even if these phrases are staples in your everyday speech, we would all do well to scrub them from our writing. This is a particular application of good advice from George Orwell. His most helpful writing tip was,

"Never use a metaphor, simile or other figure of speech which you are used to seeing in print."[5]

Reading my own work through the filter of that rule, I've realized that much of the language I use when I write about my faith, if I'm not careful, is insider language. It doesn't make sense to non-Christians. It doesn't even make sense to Christians from other denominational or cultural backgrounds. What's more, even perfectly good words can become jargon, and therefore rendered meaningless, if we use them carelessly. "Gospel" is a great noun. It's a terrible adjective. It means three different things in the following phrases: gospel music, gospel preaching, gospel leadership.

So I commend to you Orwell's rule. If you see a word or phrase in your writing that you see a lot, especially a jargony Christian word or phrase, cut it. Rephrasing it in your own words will make your writing fresh.

Remember that all these tips and rules are part of the revision process. That is, you will likely find that you have committed every one of these sins in your first draft. That's ok. Use these items as a guide for turning that lousy first draft into a document you are proud to share.

17

•

Get the Rest of Your Body Involved

Writing in a natural voice is important for every writer, and finding your voice can be a lifelong pursuit. (Personally, I don't think I'm quite there.) But it is especially important—and sometimes especially *difficult*—for people who are known for public speaking. These days it's typical for someone to become a writer because they've already become well-known as a gifted communicator. Whether pastors or professors or politicians, many speakers have an established audience who like what they have to say and like the way they say it. This makes them a publisher's dream.

But a speaker who is well-liked because they have a distinctive way of communicating can often find it difficult to translate their naturally distinctive voice from the pulpit or lectern to the printed page.

One way I find my voice in print is to read out loud everything I write. Reading aloud accomplishes several things at once. It helps me catch awkward phrasing or identify places I need to vary sentence length to maintain a readable pace. It helps me identify passages that are redundant or unnecessary. Most important for present purposes, reading aloud also helps me achieve a natural writing voice because it forces me to identify words on the page or turns of phrase I would probably not use in everyday speech. If a word feels weird coming out of my mouth—e.g., I have a hard time pronouncing it or it strikes me as pretentious—I delete it from the page.

In addition to reading with your ears, you can get the rest of your body involved. Writer Michael Perry prints his documents, tapes the pages end to end, and rolls them up like a scroll.[1] As he reads the pages aloud, he walks backwards down his hallway, unrolling the pages as he goes. If he reaches a point in the story that is confusing, where the pacing isn't right, or he has to stop reading and *think*, his scrolling stops and his body stops. This physical act helps him identify the problem spots in his writing.

Friends and family tell me that when they read my writing, they can "hear" me saying the words. This is good news. It's also really hard work. Typically, my first couple drafts of anything are stilted and unnatural. It takes several drafts before I begin to sound like myself. Typically, the first step in the right direction is when I stop writing with my eyes and start writing with my ears.

Do It: Share Your Revised Draft

Everyone can benefit from the perspective of others. In fact, you may feel you've been looking at your own words so long that you don't know if they make any sense to *you*, let alone to anyone else. It's probably a good idea to submit your revised draft to someone else before it's published, whether it's a spouse, colleague, or someone you know with writing and editing skills.

Guidelines for Good Feedback

Getting feedback is one thing. Getting *helpful* feedback is quite another. Here are some questions to ask as you seek *helpful* feedback.

1. Ask your reader what you're doing right. Is anything about the piece helpful, insightful, etc.?

2. Ask your reader to be honest. If something is unclear, redundant, or just plain wrong, you'll want to know sooner rather than later.

3. Ask your reader to be specific. Non-specific praise and critique are *both* unhelpful. Don't accept, "This is really good." Ask what is good about it. Similarly, don't accept, "Man, this is terrible." It might be terrible, but that's not helpful input. Ask for specifics.

4. Depending on how comfortable the person is doing this, ask for specific revisions. For example: "Based on your outline, it looks like you're planning to cover more material than you can address in one essay." That's good. Even better: "I recommend that you delete points two and four and focus on points

one and three. That's where you will make your most important contribution."

5. Remember to thank your reader, even if you're not thrilled with their advice. Reading your work and giving a thoughtful response takes time and care.

18

•

What's Next?

You did it. You made it to the end. (Or you skipped to the end. There's really no way for me to know.)

This short book has introduced topics and tactics that you can spend the rest of your life developing. All that's left is to ask: Where do we go from here, practically speaking?

There are more things you *could* do, but there are four things you *should* do.

First, develop writing habits.

Some people have a knack for writing, a natural talent. Some people don't. Whichever category you fit into, the only way to improve your writing is to write. And to write regularly. If you want to write better, you have to make time. Commit to writing regularly *for yourself*. Your routine may be different from mine. What works best for me is writing first thing in the morning. I (try to) wake up, shower, pour myself a cup of coffee, and write for thirty minutes. You may prefer to write at home every evening or in the office one morning per week. Consistency is more important than frequency.

Second, read more.

You won't improve as a writer if you don't write. It's equally true that you won't improve as a writer if you don't read. And *what* you read matters. Most of us these days consume a lot of content on-line—blogs, news articles, status updates, click-bait headlines. A steady diet of this sort of content can actually make us worse writers. It tempts us to imitate a chatty style and desensitizes us to jargon.

To grow as a writer, read broadly. If you are an avid reader already, and you *usually* read nonfiction, pick up a novel next. If you read a lot of fiction, pick up a good collection of essays or dive into creative nonfiction. If you usually read new releases, go read some classics. If you only read classics, go read a current bestseller. Reading widely will expand your creative vision and your vocabulary. And ultimately it will help you find your voice.

Third, start sharing your work.

Sharing doesn't require publishing. Find a few friends who will agree to read what you're writing and offer feedback. Join a writer's group that will create accountability, impose deadlines, and provide a learning community. Start an email newsletter and share your work with friends and colleagues. Writing can be lonely work. It's essential to find people to read your work and offer you feedback and encouragement.

Finally, some of you probably want to start thinking about publishing.

What I've learned in my experience as an editor and author is that it is important to go into the process with the right expectations. Anne Lamott was right: publishing won't change your life. Depending on what statistics you believe, somewhere between 600,000 and 1,000,000 new books are published in the United States *every year*. About half of those books are self-published.

Most of them sell very poorly. I don't say this to discourage you but simply to adjust your expectations. The odds of even a traditionally published author becoming rich and famous are very low. There are new magazines and journals created all the time. Many of them don't pay contributors and have low readership or circulation. The odds of going viral are very low.

None of that means you shouldn't publish. You may have an idea for a book that meets a real need in the market or fills an important gap in a niche industry or community. Even if the book is unlikely to be a commercial success, it's worth publishing if it expands your ministry, shares your expertise, and serves an audience. Just make sure you go into the process with sober expectations.

Because book publication is a goal for some, I've included a book proposal template. Even if you are considering self-publishing, creating a proposal is a helpful exercise. And not only for book projects. If you're writing an article or blog post, complete the template exercise to hone your idea.

You'll notice that the template asks for a lot of the information you've been developing throughout the exercises in this book: about your unique contribution as a writer, about your intended audience, about books (or articles) already on the market, and how your proposal fits among them. I recommend you complete a proposal for a project you have in mind. Even if you never submit it to a publisher, it will help you sharpen your thinking on the subject. I've included some notes in the proposal outline to help you apply what you've learned in previous exercises to the specific application of the proposal.

An Act of Hospitality

One my favorite lines from Charles Dickens' *A Christmas Carol* is spoken by the Ghost of Christmas Present. He invites the addled Ebenezer Scrooge into a journey with a jolly "Come inside and know me better, man!" He invites him into a Christmas feast and an evening of conversation about Scrooge's very soul.

We've considered cooking and conversation as metaphors for writing in this book. Both metaphors appeal to me for the same reason. Both, to do them right, are acts of hospitality. You take special care when you prepare a meal for guests. You consider their preferences and allergies. For their part, they arrive not so concerned about caloric intake or nutritional variety but about fun and fellowship. Likewise, the best conversations aren't primarily about exchanging information or disseminating data. They are about self-revelation, deep listening, growing intimacy.

So it is with writing. Writing is an invitation: Come inside and know me better, man! That's why even if *publishing* won't change your life, if you take the transaction seriously, writing will. Write for yourself and you will know yourself better. Write for others and you will know *them* better and your capacity for empathy will grow and grow.

That's reason enough to do the hard work. And I hope you will. We all need more good meals and conversation.

Do It: Proposal Template

Follow this format to develop a proposal for your next writing project:

Quick Facts

- Title
- Subtitle (if any)
- Author(s) Name(s)

Overview

Describe your project in two or three sentences (100 words or fewer). As efficiently as you can, tell us what the project is about, why the subject matter is important, and why you are the right author(s) to write about it.

NOTE: You can derive an overview for your project from the mission statement you developed for your work. Your mission statement will likely be in the first person ("I want to write an essay that . . ."). Revise it so that it's in the third person ("This essay . . .") and add any other information, such as your qualifications as a writer, that someone would need to understand why your project is important.

Target Audience

First, identify your primary audience. Who is most likely to benefit from this project? What problem does this project solve? Who would be most likely to purchase it or search for it? Think in terms of demographics (i.e., age, stage of life, professional responsibilities, etc.) and geography (i.e., where does the audience live, what language do they speak, etc.)

Next identify a secondary audience. What other groups and types of readers will also be interested?

NOTE: Your Identify Your Ideal Reader *exercise is great preparation for this question.*

About the Author

Tell us a little about yourself. What are your credentials and experience? What makes you uniquely qualified to write about this topic? Be creative. Provide a clear sense of your voice and values.

NOTE: *Your author bio and the* Know Thyself *exercise can provide the information you need for this section.*

Similar Titles

List any books, articles, or other resources that are similar to the one you are proposing. Briefly identify the main contribution of resources in the list. Then explain how your project is different or unique. What contribution do you make that *needs* to be made?

NOTE: *As you were conducting research for your project, you probably ran across resources that address your topic and are similar in theme or tone to your own work. The most relevant few can provide your similar titles (or "comps").*

Annotated Table of Contents

Draft a complete Table of Contents (or outline) that includes section headings or chapter titles *and* summaries of the content of each section/chapter. This section may be quite long—that's ok. Be thorough.

NOTE: *The* Reverse Outlining *exercise is a great way to generate summaries of your work.*

Recommended Resources on Writing

•

There are lots of books about writing.
Here are a few recommendations to get you started.

Always on My Desk

These are the books I keep within arm's reach for my own writing and editing:

The Chicago Manual of Style (Chicago: The University of Chicago Press, 2017). Often called by its acronym, CMS, this is the gold-standard of style guides. It's an essential resource for English grammar and usage, and it includes citation information for all sorts of resources.

Roy Peter Clark, *Writing Tools: 50 Essential Strategies for Every Writer* (New York: Little, Brown and Company, 2006). A collection of short exercises, best-practices, and advice for every part of the writing process—from planning to polishing the final draft.

Stephen King, *On Writing: A Memoir of the Craft* (New York: Pocket Books, 2000). Part memoir and part writing guide, this book is geared toward fiction writers but offers lots of helpful insights into the writing process in general. Beware of adult language.

Andrew T. Le Peau, *Write Better: A Lifelong Editor on Craft, Art, and Spirituality* (Downers Grove, IL: InterVarsity Press, 2019). Andy packs wisdom gained from more than forty years as an editor into this book, covering everything from good introductions and conclusions, the art of persuasion, and the spirituality of writing.

William Strunk Jr. and E. B. White, *Elements of Style*, Fourth Edition (New York: Longman, 2000). The classic writer's desk reference. One- and two-page pointers about style, grammar, and composition.

William Zinsser, *On Writing Well: The Classic Guide to Writing Nonfiction*, 30th Anniversary Edition (New York: Collins, 2006). If you have to start somewhere, start here. A great resource that covers the entire writing process from planning to final draft and demystifies the process along the way.

Further Reading

————————————•————————————

Robert Inchausti, ed., *Echoing Silence: Thomas Merton on the Vocation of Writing* (Boston: New Seeds, 2007). Selections from Thomas Merton's spiritual writings that speak to the Christian calling of writing.

Anne Lamott, *Bird by Bird: Some Instructions on Writing and Life* (New York: Pantheon Books, 1994). A winsome introduction to the writing process and the writing life.

Steven Pressfield, *The War of Art: Break Through the Blocks and Win Your Inner Creative Battles* (New York: Black Irish Entertainment LLC, 2012). A motivational work to give you confidence and get you to work.

Kurt Vonnegut and Suzanne McConnell, *Pity the Reader: On Writing with Style* (New York: Seven Stories Press, 2019). A collection of writing advice from novelist Kurt Vonnegut, compiled and curated by one of his former students.

Acknowledgments

———————•———————

Marshall Shelley and Skye Jethani mentored me in editorial work during our years together at Leadership Journal. They showed me that an editor's most important job is developing relationships of trust with writers. Since the writers we worked with at the time were pastors, mainly, I credit them both with instilling in me a deep appreciation for church leaders and their complicated and sensitive work of caring for souls. I've coached pastors in writing for all the years since Leadership Journal, and now it's a key part of my job for Redeemer City to City (CTC). Steve Shackelford (CEO of City to City) championed this project, and his support has ensured that the lessons I've learned through relationships with pastors around the world are finally down on paper. I'm endlessly grateful for the support of these great institutions and their leadership.

Notes

Chapter 1

1. John Jantsch, "Why Content Creation Is Everyone's Job," Duct Tape Marketing, March 3, 2018, https://ducttapemarketing.com/content-creation-everyones-job.

2. *The West Wing*, season 2, episode 9, "Galileo," directed by Alex Graves, aired November 29, 2000, on NBC.

Chapter 2

1. Attributed to Kurt Vonnegut in Anne Lamott, *Bird by Bird: Some Instructions on Writing and Life* (New York: Pantheon Books, 1994), 32.

2. William Zinsser, *On Writing Well: The Classic Guide to Writing Nonfiction*, 30th Anniversary Edition (New York: Collins, 2006), 25.

Chapter 3

1. Stephen King, *On Writing: A Memoir of the Craft* (New York: Pocket Books, 2000), 105.

2. Ibid., 106.

3. William Zinsser, *On Writing Well: The Classic Guide to Writing Nonfiction*, 30th Anniversary Edition (New York: Collins, 2006), 5.

Chapter 4

1. Kurt Vonnegut, "How to Write with Style," *IEEE Transactions on Professional Communications* PC-24, no. 2 (1981): 66.

2. Ibid.

3. Anne Lamott, *Bird by Bird: Some Instructions on Writing and Life* (New York: Pantheon Books, 1994), 185.

Chapter 5

1. Thomas Merton, *New Seeds of Contemplation* (New York: New Directions Publishing, 1972), 111.

2. Stephen King, *On Writing: A Memoir of the Craft* (New York: Pocket Books, 2000), 219.

3. Anne Lamott, *Bird by Bird: Some Instructions on Writing and Life* (New York: Pantheon Books, 1994), 185.

4. Ibid., 187.

5. Ibid., 194.

Chapter 6

1. Frank Viola, *Pagan Christianity: Exploring the Roots of Our Church Practices* (Carol Stream, IL: Tyndale Momentum, 2012), xxii–xxiv.

Chapter 7

1. Stephen King, *On Writing: A Memoir of the Craft* (New York: Pocket Books, 2000), 106, emphasis added.

2. E. B. White, "E. B. White, The Art of the Essay No. 1," interview by George Plimpton and Frank Crowther, *The Paris Review*, issue 48, Fall 1969, https://www.theparisreview.org/interviews/4155/e-b-white-the-art-of-the-essay-no-1-e-b-white.

Chapter 10

1. Andrea Beaty, *Ada Twist, Scientist* (New York: Abrams Books for Young Reader, 2016), 24.

2. Roy Peter Clark, *Writing Tools: 50 Essential Strategies for Every Writer* (New York: Little, Brown and Company, 2006), 205.

Chapter 11

1. Kurt Vonnegut, "How to Write with Style," *IEEE Transactions on Professional Communications* PC-24, no. 2 (1981): 66.

2. Quoted in Roy Peter Clark, *Writing Tools: 50 Essential Strategies for Every Writer* (New York: Little, Brown and Company, 2006), 197–98.

3. Mark Bowden, *Black Hawk Down: A Story of Modern War* (New York: Grove/Atlantic, Inc., 2010), 331–32.

4. You can read the essay that resulted from this mission statement in René Breuel, "At the Intersection of Faith and Culture: A Vision for Christian Cultural Expressiveness," *Movements of the Gospel: Experiments in Ministry in Unfamiliar Places* (New York: Redeemer City to City, 2019), 34–49.

Chapter 13

1. Anne Lamott, *Bird by Bird: Some Instructions on Writing and Life* (New York: Pantheon Books, 1994), 22.
2. Ibid., 23.

Chapter 14

1. Cal Newport, *Deep Work: Rules for Focused Success in a Distracted World* (London: Piatkus, 2016), 170.
2. Tina Fey, *Bossypants* (New York: Little, Brown and Company, 2011), 112.

Chapter 15

1. E. B. White, *The Second Tree from the Corner* (New York: Harper and Row, 1954), 158–59.
2. Ibid.
3. William Zinsser, *On Writing Well: The Classic Guide to Writing Nonfiction*, 30th Anniversary Edition (New York: Collins, 2006), 4.
4. This example is an excerpt from my article "Can You Imagine?," published online at Christian Bible Studies, *Christianity Today*, July 26, 2011, https://www.christianitytoday.com/biblestudies/articles/theology/canyouimagine.html.

Chapter 16

1. William Strunk Jr. and E. B. White, *The Elements of Style*, 4th ed. (New York: Longman, 2000), 73.
2. Ibid.
3. William Zinsser, *On Writing Well: The Classic Guide to Writing Nonfiction*, 30th Anniversary Edition (New York: Collins, 2006), 16.
4. Ibid., 15.
5. George Orwell, "Politics and the English Language," *The Collected Essays, Journalism and Letters of George Orwell* (New York: Harcourt, 1946), 139.

Chapter 17

1. I recall hearing this anecdote at an author talk in Naperville, Illinois.

REDEEMER
CITY to CITY

Redeemer City to City is a nonprofit organization that prayerfully recruits, trains, coaches, and resources leaders who cultivate gospel movements in global cities primarily through church planting. City to City is based in New York City and works in over 140 global cities throughout Africa, Asia, Australia, North America, Latin America, the Middle East, and Europe. City to City's core competencies are urban church planting, leadership development, and content creation. All of this is done to help bring the gospel of Jesus Christ to cities.

City to City was co-founded and is chaired by Tim Keller. After transitioning out of his position as senior pastor at Redeemer Presbyterian Church, Tim Keller moved into a full-time role with City to City, focusing on ministry in global cities like Johannesburg, Mumbai, London, São Paulo, and New York City. He and City to City's global leaders work together to invest in and pass along what they have learned to a new generation of ministry leaders. Through these endeavors, City to City helps build for and propel movements of the gospel in affiliate networks around the globe.

As of January 2018, City to City has helped start 495 new churches in 70 cities, trained more than 16,000 leaders in city ministry and evangelism, provided resources in 25 languages to help recruit, empower, and develop these leaders, and served 57 gospel networks around the globe.

www.redeemercitytocity.com/

 RedeemerCTC

 RedeemerCTC

 RedeemerCTC

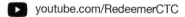 youtube.com/RedeemerCTC